SHOW US YOUR GLORY

Developing A Revival Culture

by

Tom Scarrella

Show Us Your Glory
ISBN 13: 978-1478185673
ISBN 10: 1478185678
Copyright © 2012 Tom Scarrella

Published by
Tom Scarrella Ministries
P.O. Box 9427
Fort Lauderdale, FL. 33075

Visit our Website at
www.sharethefire.org

FOREWORD

The darkness was almost tangible, the air damp and musty in the pit. I lifted my hands, straining to see even the slightest outline, but there was not a speck of light to illuminate them. With my natural senses overwhelmed, I turned to prayer. Beginning slowly pouring out my heart, I sensed another atmosphere in that hole. As my own words fell from my lips, someone else's prayers began to swirl around me and envelope me. They were 'ancient' prayers; almost oozing from the rock walls.

Intercessions of a man of God for a nation; cries for the enlightenment of a people; petitions to God for the turning of the hearts of men and woman to the True God. Continuing in this vein more intensely, I became deeply aware that a 'mantle' began to rest upon me. I was keenly aware of a spirit of revival in that strangle and to the outward senses, hostile environment. I had questions, but no answers came to mind. What was this 'experience' all about? I had no frame of reference that could explain this encounter.

Tradition has it that Bartholomew and Thaddeus preached in Armenia. But another saint, two centuries later, gained greater recognition. He was born in Armenia, but raised, in Caesarea, Cappadocia. Returning around 300 AD, Gregory began preaching in Armenia, his native land. His powerful ministry soon brought the displeasure of King Tiridates III, who had him tortured and cast into a deep pit on the Ararat Plain, under the present day church of Khor Virap, located near the historical city Artashat. Filled with dead bodies, serpents and scorpions, Gregory was condemned to remain in this confinement for between eleven to fourteen years. This saint was kept alive by a pious elderly believer, who threw bread and water into the pit, through a miniscule opening in the 'roof.'

During this time, the monarch lost his sanity and became like a wild boar roaming in the fields and forests. This reads like the familiar story of king Nebuchadnezzar in Daniel's book. The king's sisters were overheard saying "If only Gregory were alive, he would restore our brother, the King." It was made known to them that the man of God was alive. He was brought out of his dungeon. After praying for Tiridates III, the sovereign was totally restored to sanity. The royal family is converted and baptized. And Armenia becomes the first totally Christian nation.

What does a man like Gregory do for so many years, but pray? And what does he pray, but his vision? In this case, it was the conversion of a nation to God. Something of this was still 'alive,' as in 1994, centuries later, his prayers seemingly pouring out of the cavern walls, encircled me as I was praying in that very same place (2 Kings 13:21). His 'mantle' was laying there waiting for someone to pick it up. Elijah's anointing fell to the earth, not leaving with him. Elisha picked it up and continued in an increased portion of the Spirit (2 Kings chapter 2). God never intended for there to be breaches of generations, or even years between visitations or outpourings.

It was the early part of 2001, in the town of Sevan. Many pastors, prophetic and intercessory ministers were invited to a week-long conference. After an introductory message on Monday afternoon, we opened Tuesday morning's meeting with worship. As I stood in the congregation, that same mantle fell on me of seven years prior. Drunk, I began to minister and what followed can only be described as revival for that entire week. Pastors and their wives were transformed. Churches were set ablaze with the Spirit of Christ. The power was 'raw,' intense, but at the same time, so Holy. Revival broke out and overflowed into Iran and Iraq, with a knock-on effect to Armenian communities in America and other places. The Deputy President of Armenia was powerfully touched and many, even of the American Mafia, were saved.

Whatever description, title or terminology we want to apply to it, we need a move of God. We want, we need, and we have to have revival—a world changing, life transforming 'Pure God' outbreak. Without interruption; no breach to be made up (Isaiah 58:12, Ezekiel 22:30). And we are going to have them, many of them, until the crescendo that causes the Church of Jesus Christ to stand as the Perfect Man, The Bride; manifesting the fullness of Christ.

Revival mantles are aplenty. Revivalists, Reformers, Mystics, Healers and Miracle Workers—their 'garments' are still here on earth. We need to take up those 'anointings' as some have already.

I am convinced that the Gospel of the Grace of God, preached in the context of the theology of the Kingdom is an essential prelude to the greatest and lasting revival(s). Legalistic religion that condemns and preaches an escapist theology cannot invite and sustain a move of God. We can no longer invite Christ to come in reviving power, and proclaim an 'exiting' Church.

Revival is the absence of the judgment of God. It is an outpouring of His mercy on sinner and saint. We can no longer preach mixed messages of the wrath of God and revival. Mercy and condemnation are mutually exclusive. James tells us that mercy triumphs over judgment (James 2:13). Revival is the mercy of God. His goodness is His glory (Exodus 33:18-19). Signs, wonders and miracles are manifestations of the glory of Christ (John 1:14; 2:11). Revival is 'normal Christianity!'

Tom and Susie are Revivalists. They are a gift to the Body of Christ. Because of their love for Jesus Christ and His beautiful Bride, they have snatched up the 'anointed clothing' of saints now in the cloud of witnesses. They are called to teach, preach and spread Revival. Read and be ignited!

John Wasserman
Pastor of Airport Christian Fellowship
Kempton Park
South Africa

DEDICATION

I want to dedicate this book to my beautiful wife Susie. You truly are my pretty girly and I love you forever. I love you for how you tirelessly pour your heart out to see revival in the world, and that the glory of God may be poured out in every church and on every hungry heart.

I want to dedicate this book to all the revivalists that have gone before us and blazed a fiery trial of revival in the world. I dedicate this to the revival generals who endured shameful ridicule and who were wrongfully imprisoned, spat upon, and even urinated upon. They suffered as cow dung, rotten tomatoes, and eggs, were hurled at them by those in the land who stood in opposition, who could not grasp the outpouring of the glory of the Lord. We benefit today from their sacrifice and selfless pursuit to show forth His glory.

From the book of Acts to the present day, we are forever indebted to revivalists, some of whom we may never know their names, the many prayers they prayed or the sermons they preached. Yet, their impact has carved out where we are as the church of the Lord Jesus Christ.

I dedicate this book to one of my dearest friends, Rodd Bryson, who without him I would not be serving God in the ministry today. Rodd led me to Jesus in the fall of 1982. His fruit has spanned the globe and his passion for Jesus was imparted to me forever. Now, he stands with the cloud of witnesses in Heaven and cheers us on for eternity. Rodd Bryson, I hear your cheers and I will keep with all my strength that I might obtain Christ.

Lastly, I'd like to dedicate this book to all of our wonderful Scarrella Ministries partners around the world. You pray for us daily and you pour into this ministry and into our vision for revival time and time again, believing in the Word of the Lord that has burned deep in our hearts since the very beginning. May you continue to show forth His glory.

ACKNOWLEDGMENTS

I want to thank my beautiful wife, Susie, for her constant encouragement and input into this project. Your ability to capture the essence of this project in the artwork and design didn't surprise me because you are continually led by the Holy Spirit in all that you do for the Kingdom of God. We are a team in all things and I'm blessed to have you at my side every step of the way. You will always have my heart.

I want to thank Rebecca McLaughlin for her tireless work on *Show Us Your Glory* and the professionalism and integrity of her company, *Living Word Christian Publications*. The dedication and patience displayed throughout this project is nothing short of saintly. Thank you for editing the book and how you have captured the passion within the pages.

CONTENTS

PREFACE

By Tom Scarrella

"Do not think that I came to bring peace on earth. I did not come to bring peace but a sword. For I have come to 'set a man against his father, a daughter against her mother, and a daughter-in-law against her mother-in-law'; and 'a man's enemies will be those of his own household.' He who loves father or mother more than Me is not worthy of Me. And he who loves son or daughter more than Me is not worthy of Me. And he who does not take his cross and follow after Me is not worthy of Me. He who finds his life will lose it, and he who loses his life for My sake will find it. (Matthew 10:34-39 NKJV).

The word *"revival"* carries with it a connotation, that although something which was once alive is now dead, yet there is hope for new, fresh life. Many religious organizations and individuals have differing definitions of revival. Some consider it nothing more than a week of good church meetings dedicated to revival. Others define it as "hyped-up" church services that bring more money and more people into the church. A more modern characterization of revival is to publicize revival by the new manifestations of the Spirit taking place in church services. Yet, none of those descriptions have anything to do with the definition of true revival.

I remember the first time that Susie and I were invited to minister in South Africa. Encountering new cultures and new ways of life has always been very exciting to us, and South Africa was especially exciting. I was eager to try new things. One of those new things was driving on their roads. My friend, Prophet Kobus van Rensberg, handed me the keys to his car as he gave me brief driving directions to the church. He said, "Take a left out of the driveway and travel one half a kilometer before you reach the robot." I thought, "What? They have robots here in South Africa? What must I do when I reach the robot?" I was relieved to learn that in South Africa a robot is a traffic light.

Just like the robot, *revival* can mean one thing to one person and something altogether different to another. Words have different meanings and their definition can depend greatly by how they are used to relate to what being said.

Something may appear the same and yet they are thousands of miles apart. For example, the state of Florida is well known for the city of Miami with its warm sunny weather and notorious beaches. But, located in the state of Oklahoma is another city also named Miami. Both states lay claim to the city of Miami, but I assure you these two cities are quite different. Not only are they are located over 1,300 miles apart; they are also separated by totally different climates, culture, size, and people groups. They may appear to be the same, but Miami, Oklahoma is not home to warm sunny weather, nor is it home to beautiful beaches. Sometimes it is easier to define something by first determining what it is not.

Let me give you five simple statements that explains what revival is not!

1. Revival is NOT spit-flying preaching, loud worship, or healings.

2. Revival is NOT a sign posted in front of the church announcing a week of extended meetings.

3. Revival is NOT a famous evangelist preaching fiery messages on television.

4. Revival is NOT repentance.

5. Revival is NOT always comfortable.

Now that we have determined some of the things that revival is not, let me give you some clarifying statements that will help define true revival!

1. Revival IS the glory of God invading the space of the glory of man.

2. Revival means that change IS inevitable and very probable to all who welcome it.

3. Revival IS an encounter with the power of God that changes you so deeply that it affects every area of your life.

4. Revival IS often uncomfortable.

5. Revival IS usually controversial.

6. Revival IS usually offensive to the religious norm.

7. Revival IS vigorous life invading the half-dead.

8. Revival IS the power of God breathing life back into His people.

9. Revival IS often offensive (like a herd of swine running down a hill).

10. Revival IS throwing over money tables in the sanctuary and restoring the temple of God once again.

11. Revival IS the Savior of the world being birthed in a humble stable.

12. Revival IS a light to lost souls and a restoring of transparency in believers.

13. Revival IS normal Christianity.

14. Revival IS a breathing of fresh passion back into the church of Jesus Christ.

15. Revival IS a restoration of compassion toward the lost.

16. Revival IS Saul getting knocked to the ground and three days later changing everything, including his name.

17. Revival IS the reviving of purpose to the church of Jesus Christ.

My friend, I have had the privilege of going to many different places for God. I have stepped foot into many churches around the world. And as a revivalist, it is my job to take the "spiritual temperature" of every new place, and help them to meet with God where they are and then grow in His glory from that place. Some churches have grown so accustomed to the reek of religious protocol that they have become strangers to His power and presence. Revival is a foreign concept to them. But as a man of God, let me tell you that there is so much more available. There is more in God to be had. There is more in God to be done. There is more of this world to be possessed. And there is more of His glory to be shown, and it must be shown through you.

This book is purposed to not only educate you, but also inspire you and touch your spirit afresh with revival fire that will burn out anything unlike Jesus. As you turn the pages of this book, I invite you also to turn the pages of your heart and soak in a new impartation of the Holy Spirit. But be warned, the words on these pages were formed to challenge all man-made religion still left alive in your life. May you never be the same again.

ENDORSEMENTS

"Show Us Your Glory is a must read for every believer and minister of the Gospel who is hungry for Revival and change in their life, church, and ministry. This book cuts to the heart of the matter, God's Glory and the outpouring thereof. What Brother Tom has written in this book is what the church, the body of Christ, needs in this day and hour 'for such a time as this.'"

Bazil Howard-Browne
Branson, Missouri

"I have known Tom for many, many years. He is one of the most dedicated and committed revival evangelists that I know. This book will show you how to get hungry for the things of God, and run after the real and genuine instead of religion. I know from firsthand experience, my heart's cry was, *'God, Show Us Your Glory'* and He did."

Roy Fields
Lakeland, Florida

"Rev. Tom Scarrella is corporately preparing God's people with God's unusual visitations that we call Revival. You will be brought to new understanding of why things happen good and bad during and after revival. I recommend you take the time to read this great edition, *Show Us Your Glory.*"

Roberts Liardon
Sarasota, Florida

"It is an honor to write an endorsement for Tom Scarrella's new book, *Show Us Your Glory.* Tom and Susie have become good friends over the years, and they have ministered many times for us in the DSMI Center. Tom's commitment to the 'Body of Christ' and his heart to see revival invade the hearts of God's people and God's churches is powerful and refreshing. He not only carries the spirit of revival in his ministry, but he also nurtures and networks to see others understand and pursue it. This book will touch your heart as it comes from a veteran minister that seeks to touch the heart of God and partake of His mighty works."

Doug Stanton
Minneapolis, Minnesota

"*Show Us Your Glory* is a wonderful book on revival, and it's written from people who really, truly live it. I've had the pleasure of hearing Tom preach and teach about revival, and then I saw him live it outside of the pulpit! Every time Tom and Susie have ministered here in Norway, we have witnessed some of the most incredible miracles of healing, salvations, and outpourings of the Holy Ghost. This is a man and a woman of God who clearly know their God and who are clearly known *by* their God, with signs and wonders following their ministry. I whole-heartily endorse this book and their ministry."

Evangelist/Pastor Rolf Auke
Tonsberg, Norway

"What is Revival? Many go around today conducting revivals, but they really have no idea what true revival is all about. They hold meetings and call it revival simply because 'revival' has become the popular *buzz* word in Christianity. But, revival is so much more. If ever there was a time for individuals to be baptized in the Fire of God, with something tangible from God, it is now. This is why I recommend Tom's book, *Show Us Your Glory*. Tom understands revival, and he understands that it comes from experience. Revival is not a sermon; revival is a returning to our First Love. I have had the opportunity to conduct revival meetings alongside Tom, and I highly recommend his ministry and this book."

Evangelist Richard Moore
Tampa, Florida

CHAPTER 1
SHOW US
YOUR GLORY

"And it came to pass, when Moses entered the tabernacle, that the pillar of cloud descended and stood at the door of the tabernacle, and the Lord talked with Moses. So the Lord spoke to Moses face to face, as a man speaks to his friend... I pray, if I have found grace in Your sight, show me now Your way, that I may know You and that I may find grace in Your sight... For how then will it be known that Your people and I have found grace in Your sight, except You go with us?... So the Lord said to Moses, 'I will also do this thing that you have spoken; for you have found grace in My sight, and I know you by name.' And he said, Please, show me Your glory. Then He said, I will make all My goodness pass before you..." (Exodus 33:9, 15)

To have God's glory, His presence must be your priority and its pursuit more important than anything else. Moses was hungry for God's glory. He was desperate for God's presence and he said to God, *"Show me Your way that I may know You! Show me Your glory."*

In 1982, I was gloriously born again, and in 1983, I was baptized with the Holy Spirit speaking in other tongues. While many of my friends either backslid or their fire for Christ had cooled off, I was still burning hotter than ever and was full-time in the ministry by 1986. After pastoring in New Jersey and California, I transitioned to become an evangelist in Tulsa, Oklahoma in 1994. After two semi-successful years of the traveling ministry, I have seen miracles and many salvations everywhere I traveled, but soon I found myself in a new place, longing for something deeper and more powerful.

I can remember the exact day and time when I was overcome with desperate hunger for God's glory. I begged God to burn everything out of me that was offensive to Him. I had become broken in the system of dead religion, and I could no longer tolerate all the religious garbage with which I had been living. I wanted change and I knew that the change needed to begin first in me. I hungered for an increase of signs and wonders in my ministry. I wanted to preach the Word of God with conviction instead of condemnation. I longed to preach from my heart instead of my head. I wanted to experience the presence of God and I needed God to show me His glory. It was then in my struggle and desperation that God changed everything. God brought radical change to my life and ministry. I couldn't stand behind a pulpit without manifesting a demonstration of God's glory in the meetings. I had prayed just as Moses prayed. And God responded to me just as He had responded to Moses.

The Bible tells us that the Lord told Moses to depart to the land that He promised, and it was a land flowing with milk and honey.

"Then the Lord said to Moses, "Depart and go up from here, you and the people whom you have brought out of the land of Egypt, to the land of which I swore to Abraham, Isaac, and Jacob, saying, 'To your descendants I will give it.' And I will send My Angel before you... Go up to a land flowing with milk and honey ...." (Exodus 33:1-3 NKJV).

God's glory will show up when His presence fills you. When Moses went into the tabernacle, God's glory descended as a pillar of a cloud and all the children of Israel were witness to it.

"All the people saw the pillar of cloud standing at the tabernacle door, and all the people rose and worshiped, each man in his tent door" (Exodus 33:10 NKJV).

Moses cried out to God with desperation and said, *"Please, show me Your glory!"* God said, *"I will make all My goodness pass before you..."* Moses sounds like a hungry person who wanted the glory and presence of God in his life. God's response to a hungry person was so simple, *"I will make My goodness pass before you..."* It all begins with hunger and it all ends with God's goodness. When you are hungry for the presence of God, then God will show you His goodness in such a new and wonderful way. THAT IS REVIVAL!

2

There Must Be More

That time of great change in my life and ministry started when I received a prophetic word from Kenneth Hagin, Jr., who was my pastor. I was traveling as an evangelist out of Tulsa, Oklahoma and *Rhema Bible Church* was my home church. I was off the road for a couple of days, and I wanted to go to my own church to receive from the Lord before I had to leave for my next ministry engagement scheduled in Minneapolis, Minnesota. That Wednesday night in early February of 1998, as Pastor Kenneth Hagin Jr. was preparing to preach, I couldn't help but notice that he kept looking over in my direction and he hesitated several times to begin his sermon.

That night, there were over 2,500 people in attendance. He finally yielded to his hesitation as I heard him say, "Tom Scarrella, come down here to the front." I quickly obeyed and came down to the front while he introduced me to the congregation as an evangelist from that church. Then he began to prophesy. He prophesied about the coming changes that were to take place in my ministry. He spoke of how God was about to flip the whole ministry right side up. Overwhelmed by what God was speaking through my pastor, I just stood there as the warm tears rolled down my face. He ended by saying, "God has heard your cries of hunger. Get ready. Very quickly your ministry will change and a spirit of revival is about to hit it in a dramatic way."

Early the next morning I packed and got into my van to begin the long drive from Tulsa to Minneapolis. I popped in a new worship album I had just purchased called, *Brownsville Worship 2.* I wasn't out of my town before I began to shake in the seat of my van with tears filling my eyes. The song was called, *"There Must Be More."* I immediately recognized the words of the song – they had been my prayer to God for so long. These were the words written on the very inner depths of my soul. Little did I know that this one song was about to set the course for the next ten years of my life and ministry. God was preparing me for this next step up into a higher place. Mile after mile and hour after hour, I listened to that one song for the entire eleven-hour drive. Finally, I felt, there really is something more, something tangible. Was this revival?

3

Not Church as Usual

Let me share what happened when I first saw God's glory revival flood a congregation, and it was not church as usual any longer. You see, when people are hungry for God's glory, it is then that His presence and power will fill a place. I had ministered at this church several times over the last two years but from the moment I arrived, I could tell that something was different—something had changed these people. The pastor shared with me how the entire church had taken over ten trips to the *Toronto Blessing* in Ontario, Canada, and to Pensacola, Florida where the *Brownsville Revival* was poured out. He went on to share about the *Smithton Outpouring*, the place where they had gone and experienced the greatest transformation as a church. For the last six months, the church had traveled fourteen times to the *Smithton Outpouring* in Smithton, Missouri. I had never heard of such desperation taking place that an entire congregation would rearrange their work schedules and sacrifice their family vacation to drive hundreds of miles away just to experience the power of God being poured out in another man's church.

Our conversation lasted for hours as he passionately shared with me about what they had experienced in revival and about all that God was doing in their personal lives and in their corporate church family. My spirit was leaping within me as I hung on his every word.

It was with expectation and anticipation for God's presence that we entered the church building that night. We arrived one hour before the meeting, and much to my amazement, the whole church of about 200 people were already there. They were gathered together in the front of the church sanctuary, and together they were interceding for the week of meetings that were to begin that night. In one corporate voice they cried out in prayer for the power and presence of God. They asked God to touch and change the life of every visitor who would be coming throughout the week. I turned to the soundman and asked him if I had misunderstood the time that the meeting was supposed to start. He was quick to respond with a smile saying, "No, we all come one hour early to prepare the atmosphere for the power of God to flow easier to the people of God." What? I had never heard of ANY church coming early just to pray—and pray they did.

There was not one head buried in a pew—not one person dozing off asleep. Instead, with tears running down their faces and passion in their voices, they sought after the presence of God, if not for their own benefit, but for the benefit of those yet to come from the surrounding area. The outside temperature was below zero, but their hunger was at a red-hot melting point. I was so moved by the Holy Spirit as their cries could be heard from out into the street. Yes, this was revival. I had never seen anything like in all my life. Soon, I heard the worship begin in the sanctuary. The pastor and I walked into the meeting. By now, not only was the whole church present, but visitors were filing in from all over the city.

One by one the congregation came out of their seats and up to the front of the church to worship the Lord. They worshiped Him with all their might, their hands raised high and their voices raised higher. The passion of the people wrecked me. Where was this intensity of passion in worship and prayer coming from? I was mesmerized. Their zeal erupted from each person's voice. Demonstrative worship was the norm and not the exception. They had something I longed to have and oh how I was desperate to experience it and bring it all over the world. After two and a half hours of passionate, reckless, God-centered worship, I stood up to preach; my legs were weak and wobbly from the presence of God. A fear of God was in the atmosphere and as I started preaching I was moved into tears as the presence of God was swirling around me like a cyclone in the building.

Offended by the Spirit of God

I'm not sure how, but I managed to deliver my sermon. When I gave the altar call for salvation, I closed my eyes to pray for the lost to be saved. I did not expect what happened next. With my eyes shut to pray I went into a vision. What I saw stunned me. I saw myself standing at the foot of the mount of transfiguration. But instead of seeing Jesus, Moses, and Elijah, I saw Jesus, Kenneth Hagin, and Kenneth Copeland. Then the voice of God thundered and said, *"Tom, You gave a place in your heart to these men that I never told*

5

you to give them. THIS [Jesus] is my beloved Son. Hear Him!" While the power of God was reverberating through me I could feel my body begin to shake heavily. The vision continued, and the next thing I saw was me standing in the front altar while a prayer team from the church circled around me praying. Then the vision was over.

Instantly I began to reason with myself. I thought, "This cannot be God because I just drove eleven hours to minister to these people. After all, I'm the guest evangelist! What will they think?" But, the Lord was clear in His request and I knew that. I turned to the pastor and inquired for him to allow me to obey the Lord in this vision. The Pastor's response was that of grace and he said, "Tom, we've all been in your place. No one will think a thing. They know that you're hungry for more of God. Go, get filled up."

It was all I could do to walk off the podium and to the front altar area. Just as in the vision, a team of prayer ministers surrounded me, and oh, the glory I felt in that moment. The presence of the living God washed over me—body and soul. As the prayer team prayed, the power of God hit me harder than ever before. I felt the strongest anointing I had ever felt in my life, until that time. I stood before Jesus shaking, vibrating, and weeping so fiercely that my nose literally began to bleed, and still I wept.

Hour upon hour I wept in the glory of God. I was still in the altar long after the meeting had concluded, and most everyone had left the building. I could not stop weeping for the fire off the altar of God was burning through me. One of the ushers helped me back to the place where I was staying, but I continued weeping even into the next day.

I wept for four days straight, only able to stop long enough to preach each night. I thought that I may not survive this heavy current of God's power as it coursed through me. I could not even feel my body for those four days as the fire burned hotter, transforming every part of me. God was busy burning the years of religious trash out from my heart and mind. Finally, that wicked root of lukewarm Christianity was leaving me for good.

"When you have been touched with fire, you hate the smell of smoke." — Dr. Rodney Howard-Browne[1]

When the four days of the fire were over, I was different. From that day forward, I was no longer an arrogant need-of-nothing Christian. Instead, I was quick to repent and my heart was so softened that it didn't take more than the first chord to be stuck in worship before I would weep anew. For years following this incident, there were many times that I would step up to preach, and great conviction would fall before I could speak a word. Several times, people got up unprovoked and publicly repented of their sins; others would wept and cry in the presence of God.

So many people and churches proudly declare that their church or ministry is in revival, and yet there is no spirit of hunger anywhere. They are convinced that they have revival, but humility is the farthest thing from sight. Revival is embroidered on their church banners, but their hearts are not soft and teachable. Fire is meant to burn. It's meant to literally consume everything with which it comes into contact. Once the old is burned away, then new growth can spring forth. It is time to get our eyes back on Jesus, for it is when we see the Lord that all things become clear in our lives. When we see Jesus, we have a clearer understanding and the motives of our hearts are laid bare under the presence of our Masterful grace Giver.

Wrecked for Religion

The next week I drove back home to Tulsa. I thought all my colleagues and pastor friends would be excited about this new found reviving fire I had embraced in my heart and life. When I tried to explain what had happened to me, strangely, some of my friends thought I had flipped my lid and had gone off the deep end of the Charismatic pool. In fact, one of my closest friends, at the time, took me aside to convince me to "calm down" by telling me that he had revival too, even though it looked different in him because he was able to bring it under control. It did not take very long, and one by one, they would turn their hearts from me.

"It's hard to have revival if you think you are in revival." – Dr. Rodney Howard-Browne[2]

I was so wrecked for anything less than the tangible presence of God's reviving power. I no longer had room for religious rituals and the lifeless routine of "church as normal." To many people, I had become far too narrow-minded to believe that there was no Truth outside of revival in the Bible. I began to see it everywhere throughout church history. The early church was passionate for the fire of the glory of God. They cried out in their hearts just like Moses did when he said, "Lord, show us your glory!" In the church today, there are some who want to reap the *dividends* of revival and enjoy the benefits of it without walking in the cost of revival, which is simple—your entire heart for His.

> *"So the Lord spoke to Moses face to face, as a man speaks to his friend... I pray, if I have found grace in Your sight, show me now Your way"* (Exodus 33:11, 13 NKJV).

There is a discovery of revival and a revelation of it that can only be revealed by the Spirit of God. Many ministers and theologians have tried to make reason of revival. Usually, it is put down as something that is everywhere at every time. But look around. If that were the truth then why is the average church in America and in other nations full of apathy and dullness? The revelation of revival can only be discovered by the *humble* and *hungry* heart. The arrogant and self-satisfied will miss it every time. Those who think that they already have revival will miss it by a mile because they are no longer in *search* of it and they no longer treasure it as their highest valuable. The Bible speaks much about searching, knocking, seeking and finding.

> *"If you seek her as silver, And search for her as for hidden treasures; Then you will understand the fear of the Lord, And find the knowledge of God"* (Proverbs 2:4-5 NKJV).

> *"It is the glory of God to conceal a matter, But the glory of kings is to search out a matter"* (Proverbs 25:2 NKJV).

> *"In that hour Jesus rejoiced in the Spirit and said, "I thank You, Father, Lord of heaven and earth, that You have hidden these things from the wise and prudent and revealed them to babes. Even so, Father, for so it seemed good in Your sight"* (Luke 10:21 NKJV).

Why would God hide things from one group only to reveal things to another group? The answer is so simple. God wants *humble* and *hungry* people who are willing to dedicate their lives to the pursuit of Him. And He promises that those who seek Him will indeed, find Him.

The Case of the Rotting Carcass

"Religion is like bad breath; most don't know that they have it on them!" – Dr. Rodney Howard-Browne[3]

For several year in a row, we would be asked to minister in the central part of Pennsylvania for our friend, Pastor Dale. Dale was an elderly man and he and his wife, Claire, had become good friends of ours over the years. He had a thriving congregation in a fairly small town, and we were always glad to reconnect and minister for our friends.

During one of our annual ministry engagements, Pastor Dale told me a story of something that had happened to him just earlier in the week. He told me that in his hunger to spiritually prepare for our coming, each night he would go to the church and pray through the night. He challenged his whole church to fast and pray in anticipation for what the Lord might do in our meetings to come the following week. One of the nights early in the week he had supper with Claire and then jumped into his car and headed to the church to pray all night. He arrived at the church and went in to pray. He prayed, especially that night, that the hearts of the people would be set right before God. About an hour into his prayer vigil a foul odor began to fill the sanctuary. Curiously, he got up and searched around for the source of the offensive aroma. He finally looked out of the side door of the church, and there laid a disgusting sight. In the driveway of the church, was the rotting carcass of a dead woodchuck. Pastor Dale was so appalled that his leaders had not cleared the dead animal off the pavement before that night. He said that it clearly had been lying in the driveway rotting for days.

Pastor Dale did not want to wait for someone else to get a shovel and throw it into the woods, so he made his way through the darkness into the storage shed behind the church and found a shovel. And all the while, he grumbled and complained under his breath why no one cared to clean up this mess before the smell became so rank that it found its way into the house of God. The closer that Pastor Dale came to the dead remains, the greater the stench became.

Covering his nose and mouth, Pastor Dale took the shovel, scooped up the polluted carcass and to his amazement, in that moment the Spirit of God spoke to him. He heard the words of the Lord so clear, "This is what your church smells like to me." With the rotting animal still teetering on the edge of the shovel, Pastor Dale broke down weeping. He dropped the shovel and fell to his knees as the presence of God overwhelmed him in intercession. God was preparing him for what was about to break forth in those meetings the following week.

For the first time, Pastor Dale realized the genuine need for revival. Revival would be for him and for those who were hungry enough to follow him into the flames of God. Sadly, it's been my experience that many churches look and smell exactly like that dead rotting carcass. But, when we allow the Holy Spirit to pull the covers off of our minds and the religious blinders from our eyes, we will be in position for a great and life-lasting move of God.

Revival is not man's idea, but it is God's idea. When we realize that God wants to pour out on the church like in the days of the Acts of the Apostles, we must cry out as Moses cried out, "Show me your way!"

"I pray, if I have found grace in Your sight, show me now Your way..." (Exodus 33:13 KJV).

God's way is revival! God's way is His power and presence in full manifestation in every service, even during a Sunday morning service. From revival we become transformed into the revival, and we are able to manifest the power of God by the Holy Spirit anytime and anywhere to anyone. God is ready and willing to change everything in you. He is ready and willing to turn you into the radical revivalist you were always meant to be, with the demonstration of His glory that will flow in you and then out of you, commanding change in the lives of countless others. That is revival and the goodness of God passing before you. Grab hold of it today. Don't put it off until tomorrow. He is ready and willing. Are you?

CHAPTER 2
QUIT PLAYING
IN YOUR FOOD

"Blessed are those who hunger and thirst for righteousness, for they shall be filled" (Matthew 5:6 KJV).

When we stop playing church and actually get hungry for God, there will be an awesome revival of God's presence in our midst. The Bible tells us that God fills the hungry and thirsty. Our pursuit of God is as simple as that.

If there has ever been a time when the church needs the presence of God, it is the hour with which we live. Many in the church have lost the presence of God and have fallen by the wayside of religious dead works. Many busy themselves playing the game of church, void of any hunger for God. Yet, there are still others who are starving for God's presence and to them, nothing else matters, and nothing else will satisfy their deep hunger pangs.

Just as the deep cries out unto the Deep, I pray that you will be counted among those going after God's presence, letting no distractions steal away your gaze upon the Christ.

As a young boy, I grew up in a very small country town on the prairie plains of Western Minnesota. My mother was a caring single mom for many years until she remarried a wonderful man who took on the challenge of raising a very mischievous me.

My mother did not let me get away with anything and let me tell you, she was always watching. One night, my friends were calling me to come out to play and race our bikes up and down the driveway. We had already built jumps and it was going to be fun. Before I could join my friends, my mother told me that all I had to do was to finish my supper. Mom was always an incredible cook; however, I had a love for fun, and an equal hatred for eating my vegetables.

That night, mom dished up a delightful home cooked meal of meat, potatoes and gravy, and a large helping of peas. The mound of peas seemed to me like kryptonite to superman, and they all but took my breath away. My mother's instruction rang out again, "You can go outside and play after all of those peas are gone." As her words permeated the air, I quickly took my spoon and scooped up a large helping of peas with a look of disgust. As the peas neared my mouth, one fell off, rolled under the plate and completely out of view. The light bulbs went off in my seven-year-old brain, and I reminded myself what she had said, "… until all the peas are gone."

As she turned to begin cleaning the stack of dishes in the sink, I began my task by quickly shoving all the peas under the plate, packing them tightly out of view. I stood up and announced, "I'm finished with all the peas. Now I'm going out to play." My mother nodded as I ran outside and played for a few hours with the fellas. We laughed as we popped wheelies, and jumped our bicycles off the ramps, completely oblivious to the wrath that lurked ahead of me.

As it got a little later, I knew that I had to go inside and get ready for bed. I walked up the stairs unknowing of what was to befall me. In my mind, I had found the solution of the ages and solved my problem with vegetables forevermore. All was well in my seven-year-old world, but I was walking into an ambush.

As I opened the front door I greeted my mother. Her head turned to me and with one glance of her eye; I knew that my sin had found me out. She asked me how the peas were tonight, and I answered her the best answer I could think of, "They were okay." She came over to me and said, "Tom, you must learn to stop playing in your food!" That night, there was a weeping and gnashing of teeth as I received the punishment for my transgression.

Thirsty at the River

Desperate people do desperate things. This is especially true when there is a starving for the power and presence of God deep in the heart of man. That starvation can reach the point when you willingly rearrange your life for its complete accommodation. In that place, there is no room for other agendas. Substandard motives surface to the top and are eagerly confronted and overcome, and in the midst of it all is an ultimate yielding to the desire and direction of God.

In the book of Judges, the Lord told Gideon to test the people by bringing them down to the water's edge to observe by which fashion the men drank from the stream. Among them would be those who would lap the water. It would be by these men that God would win the battle. They were thirsty for the water and open for change by the Spirit of God.

> *"But the Lord said to Gideon, "The people are still too many; bring them down to the water, and I will test them for you there. Then it will be, that of whom I say to you, 'This one shall go with you,' the same shall go with you; and of whomever I say to you, 'This one shall not go with you,' the same shall not go." So he brought the people down to the water. And the Lord said to Gideon, "Everyone who laps from the water with his tongue, as a dog laps, you shall set apart by himself; likewise everyone who gets down on his knees to drink"* (Judges 7:4-5 NKJV).

Hungry people are unpredictable, and truly thirsty people will stop at nothing to quench their thirst in order to sustain them another day. Governments and heads of states fear few things, but one thing they do fear are hungry people in the time of famine and thirsty people in the time of drought. The masses revolt, minor wars break out, and governments have been overthrown when people rise up during times of great physical hunger, famine, and drought. While these are the result of natural starvation and hunger, imagine the willingness of a gracious God when His children become thirsty in the dry and weary lands where there is no water.

Nathan's Rescue

> *"On the last day, that great day of the feast, Jesus stood and cried out, saying, "If anyone thirsts, let him come to Me and drink. He who believes in Me, as the Scripture has said, out of his heart will flow rivers of living water"* (John 7:37-38 NKJV).

13

Sitting in my office one day, my wife came to me with a letter that the ministry received from a young man living in the state of Kansas. Correspondences are usually handled by my wife and she personally responds to each letter and email we receive, but this letter was different. The letter began with the usual formalities, but he quickly dove into his story of desperation. His name was Nathan and he was 16 years old. He had somehow gotten hold of one my sermons on cassette from years ago, and on it he heard me telling my story of coming to Jesus—and a young boy myself.

He was inspired and Nathan decided to write and ask me for my advice. Saved just six months before, he explained that he was now fasting to get closer to the Holy Spirit. He explained how he felt that he was spiritually starving because something deep, deep within him wanted more and more of the things of God. Nathan had grown up in an extremely abusive family. His mother would often leave for extended periods of time, leaving him in the care of his cruel step-father and older brothers. By the age of nine years, Nathan had endured every abuse you can imagine, and as I read his letter, I could not help but break down.

Very sincerely, he shared with me about the family he had been sent to live with—his foster family. His foster mom, Georgina, was a soft spoken woman with a very loud love for God. Because of their love for children, Georgina, and her husband, Peter, turned to foster care. Nathan was not accustomed to kind, gentle words and admitingly, he pushed his boundaries with them at first. But each night in bed, he would lay awake listening to Georgina pray, and cry out to God to help Nathan and to help make her a good mom to him.

Finally, one night Nathan sat up in bed. He was overcome by the "feeling" of something he had never experienced. He wondered what it was. The next thing he knew—Jesus appeared before him. He was wearing blue jeans and a t-shirt. He sat at the edge of Nathan's bed and He rested one hand on Nathan's foot. Trying to adjust his eyes, Nathan watched as a dark shadow came out from his chest. At the same time, a bright white light entered. Then just as suddenly as Jesus had appeared to him, He was gone.

That night had occurred six month earlier, and now Nathan was hungrier to know Jesus than ever before. He shared his experience with Georgina, and together they set out to fast and seek God for the infilling of the Holy Spirit. He was willing to do whatever it took to get more of God in his life, he explained. He felt that he was called to preach, and he sought my advice on what he should do to get started. WOW! What type of advice could I give him that the Holy One hadn't already given him in that one life-changing encounter?

Get the Camera Lady God!

Several years ago while ministering out west, I was invited to appear on a major Christian television station, which is one of the largest in the world. They asked me to speak from my heart, so I introduced the viewers to revival, and I began to preach about being hungry for more of Jesus. I explained to them that the enemy of revival is apathy and self-satisfaction. I said, "Even though a person can be swimming in the ocean, there remains the possibility that they could die of thirst." Likewise, many people are in the church, but they are not hungry or thirsty for more.

I was only given a fifteen-minute time slot to minister, and I wanted to make it a dynamo to get people hungry for the presence and power of God. That day, there were a few people in the studio. As I began to speak about revival and hunger, I looked around and noticed that all the camera people were weeping. One lady in particular was weeping so hard that she began to sob and shake under the glory of God. The longer I began to tell about the condition of the church worldwide and how we must passionately hunger for the presence of God, the harder she shook. She shook for those fifteen-minutes, and by the end, we had to have someone sit her down on a chair because she was so lost in the glory of God.

After the filming, she told me that she had never been told that she even needed to be hungry or passionate for the power of God in her whole Christian life. In that television studio, she became broken and humble in the presence of God. The power and glory of God had manifested in her so much so that she was unable to drive herself home that day from the studio.

This Current Sickness

Worldwide, the church of Jesus Christ is so sick today. She does not know that she needs to be hungry. Very few church leaders care enough about the people or the Holy Spirit to tell the people that spiritually they need to get hungry and thirsty. For the sake of not causing offense, many pastors and church leaders avoid the matter of hunger while continuing on with the regular church programs, pageants, and church picnics. For some time now, the church of Jesus Christ looks and functions more like a social club than a red-hot burning, power-filled fortress to the world.

Spiritual urgency is birthed out of spiritual hunger. When someone does not recognize the symptoms of a sickness and they are unfamiliar with the effects of the sickness, they go on believing they are healthy and whole, when, in reality, they are in trouble!

"Then the men of the city said to Elisha, "Please notice, the situation of this city is pleasant, as my lord sees; but the water is bad, and the ground barren." And he said, "Bring me a new bowl, and put salt in it." So they brought it to him. Then he went out to the source of the water, and cast in the salt there, and said, "Thus says the Lord: 'I have healed this water; from it there shall be no more death or barrenness.' "So the water remains healed to this day, according to the word of Elisha which he spoke" (II Kings 2:19-22 NKJV)?

Notice the words, *"... but the water is bad, and the ground barren....put salt in it."* There had to be some urgency, some immediate need with Elisha to do something about a polluted spring of water. The Bible doesn't say that Elisha waited awhile before he acted as a man of God. No, right then and there, he put salt in a new bowl, and cast it into the water so that the waters could be healed.

Today in this hour, many major leaders do not know that the water of the church is bad. They do not recognize the symptoms or the sickness causing the symptoms. There are major denominations that neglect and even deny the gift of speaking in tongues. Some avoid the subject of casting out devils. On global television, certain major Christian leaders are afraid to say that Jesus Christ is the ONLY way. They do not know that they are really sick.

The sickness overtaking the church of Jesus Christ is so rank and pitiful that it would make great men of old, like Martin Luther and John Wesley, disgusted. Personally I know of major ministries that for decades, have purposely hidden and covered up sin within their family for fear that the money would dry up. Their children are like the sons of Eli; there is no spirit of revival in the air, and the atmosphere is as plastic as spiritual Tupperware.

Hunger Humbles

When a person is hungry for the outpouring of the Holy Spirit, it brings humility to that person, and a desire to be taught by the Spirit of God. Hungry people do not want to fight over the color of the carpet in the sanctuary, the choir's robes, or where to spend the money someone willed to the church.

Hungry people just want God's presence. They don't want to talk about the devil and what he's doing, but they want to talk about God and what He's doing. They don't want to spend their prayer time yelling at satan, but they want to spend that time with the One that they love, the Lord Jesus Christ.

Hunger is what sets the bar for your spirituality. Your hunger is like the sights of a gun that has an aim. The sight sets the point of the direction of the bullet. At the end of our revival meetings, it is common for me to walk back into the sanctuary and see the saints that are still on the floor; some have tears in their eyes, and some are crying out to God with all their heart. These are the spiritual ones.

Nothing touches my heart like hunger in God's people. I just love to look at the faces as their hearts are engaged with the power of God, and the Holy Spirit is searching the deep things of their spirit. I know that change is happening in their minds and hearts. They are connecting spirit to spirit and mind to mind with Holy Spirit of God.

My wife and I agree that we would rather minister to a person hungry for the Holy Spirit than just about anything else. In the altar time, we would rather stay to minister to the hungry than rush off to the back with the other ministers. When they try to rush us out, we have had to tell them to leave without us as we were doing the Master's business. We were born for this purpose, and that is to make people hungry and keep them hungry because hunger is a sign of life.

"It's a scary sight to walk into most Sunday morning services." – Dr. Rodney Howard-Browne[4]

In California during the late 1990s, I was invited to be the guest minister for a church that was celebrating their 25th year anniversary. Before the first night of the church anniversary conference, I was pulled aside by the senior pastor and told that after praise and worship was finished, I would be given the microphone. He said that I would have only thirty minutes to preach. He explained that he had already told the praise and worship team to cut it short, because he knew that many of the people wanted to leave early and go to the restaurant. As I took the microphone that night, the Spirit of the Lord had me tell the people to quit playing in their food. As I continued, it was as if the glory of God ripped through the church like a knife, revealing those who were hungry from those who were ready to go to the restaurant and eat.

Suddenly the youth and young adults, in the church, ran to the front by the dozens, weeping under the power of God. Soon their weeping became contagious. In particular, one man stood out to me as I watched the glory of God swept through that building; within moments, this masculine man fell on the floor, weeping and crying at the top of his lungs. People around him were shocked because they had never seen this big man so much as shed a single tear, much less weep and cry out in this manner.

After the service, a young man from the youth group came up to me and hugged me. I asked him, "What happened to you tonight?" He quickly answered, "I had a vision for the first time in my life. And in the vision, I had shackles on my feet, but Jesus Christ walked to me and broke them with His hammer. When the shackles fell from

18

my feet, I was more free than I have ever known before, and all I want to do is worship Him and serve Him."

God does not lie. He fills the hungry with good things, and it is the goodness of God that gently leads us to the place of repentance where we grow in His ways. He is no respecter of persons. What He has done in the lives of others, He will do for you when you set your hungry heart to seek Him.

CHAPTER 3
WHAT MUST WE DO?

Revival is certainly a spiritual matter, but it is very much a natural matter also. There are very practical, natural things that we can do to have life-changing revival. Revivals begin and sadly revivals end. Like a campfire, there are practical things you can do, like stoking the flames or adding more fuel in order to keep the fire burning longer and hotter; likewise, there are things you can do to extinguish the flames completely. Whether intentional or unintentional, the outcome of our actions will surely affect the revival flow in our lives and in our churches.

So, what must we do to start revival? It may sound carnal to ask such a question. The truth is, it is carnal, but remember, since the beginning of time, God has used fleshly man to do godly things. Moses parted the Red Sea, Esther saved her people, and Noah built an ark before the earth had ever experienced rain fall. Sampson single-handedly slaughtered the thousands, David defeated the giant with stones, and Peter walked on water and drew money from the mouth of fish. It was in the hands of the disciples that he loaves and fishes were multiplied.

In I Chronicles, Uzza learned quickly that natural man was created to carry the presence of God on his shoulders, not the oxen.

Starting a revival begins by looking into the mirror. For a pastor to start revival, he must first have revival himself. From there, revival will trickle down to the church. The humble heart can have revival. The hungry heart can *catch* the spirit of revival by going to where the fire is already burning.

To start a genuine life-changing revival in your life and church, motives must be right, and among them are hunger, humility, integrity in money and the flexibility to flow with change.

Revival Starts In the Leaders
Before It Trickles Down to the Church

We were scheduled to minister each night for an entire week at a small church in Shelbyville, Indiana, which is about thirty minutes just south of Indianapolis. We arrived the day before and the pastor and his wife invited us out to dinner for a chance to get to know each other before the start of the week meetings. As we ate, we fellowshipped and after some small-talk, he and his wife began to pour out their hearts, even confiding in us that they were thinking of resigning from ministry altogether.

At first, they sounded like desperate pastors who had grown discouraged by the lack of Christian enthusiasm in their church – a situation I've heard many times before from many pastors. But, as the week went on, we realized that we had mistaken desperation for something much different.

"We want revival, but we're tired of trying to get our leaders enthusiastic again about revival. We are worn-out from trying to encourage the people to come to prayer meetings. And the worship team—that's another story." he explained. With such statements, we assumed that that they were hungry for change and willing to do something different. Perhaps they were open and teachable to some good and wise counsel, or so I thought.

One night in the middle of the week, after the meeting ended, I took the opportunity to share with the pastor some of the things that I observed throughout the week. I agreed with him that there was a problem with his church leaders, especially considering that not one of them bothered to attend any of the week's meetings. I proceeded to tell him that despite the current apathy, revival was still very possible for them, and that the best way to begin is by allowing revival to start in he and his wife first. I explained to him that revival will flow down from the leadership head and then into the people.

Catch Revival By Going
Where the Fire is Burning

One of the best ways to *catch* revival in your church is to go where the fire is already burning. I told these pastors about the fires raging in Pensacola, Florida; Toronto, Canada; Tampa, Florida; and in Smithton, Missouri. I encouraged them to do whatever it took to get to one or more of these outpourings. The pastor arrogantly replied, "We shouldn't have to go anywhere to get revival. God is here in Shelbyville too."

They did not want to even entertain the reality that perhaps they needed to go somewhere else to get hold of revival. I am certainly blessed that the wise men, spoken of in the Bible, didn't share that opinion. The Bibles says, they traveled to find the Christ child. They obviously didn't wait for Him to come to them. If they had waited for Him to come to them, I think they would have been waiting a very, very long time.

You see, many people want revival in their church as long as they do not have to give up anything or do anything differently.

But, I was there to help show them a better way. The Truth is always a help, even if hearing it offends our mind. I reminded the pastor what Mary, the mother of Jesus, said to the angel of the Lord in the book of Luke, *"Be it unto ME even according to your word"* (Luke 1:38 NKJV).

I guess they weren't so humble or teachable after all, because their offense rose up at the slightest insinuation that they needed to be the first to change, and that traveling to where the fire was poured out may be the best way to catch the fire and bring it back to Shelbyville. The pastor was right. God was right there in Shelbyville too. But, God was not in manifestation in their church like He was at those other places.

How Do You Start Revival?

"Then he fell to the ground, and heard a voice saying him, "Saul, Saul, why are you persecuting Me?" And he said, "Who are You, Lord?" Then the Lord said, "I am Jesus, whom you are persecuting. It is hard for you to kick against the goads." So he, trembling and astonished, said, "Lord, what do You want me to do?" Then the Lord said to him, "Arise and go into the city, and you will be told what you must do" (Acts 9:4-6 NKJV).

23

Paul, the Apostle, began his life known as Saul. He was a Jewish Pharisee, and he was doing all that he could do to bring persecution to the Christian followers. As he walked on the Damascus road, he experienced a powerful encounter with Jesus. Suddenly, he was face to face with the very One whose followers he was determined to destroy, the Son of the Living God. Stopped by the power of God, Paul's swift and urgent response was simply, "Lord, what do You want me to do?" By this response, we can easily conclude that Paul had a genuine change of heart that day.

Paul's experience, on that day, is a great example of how we too can position ourselves for revival. Paul was immediately humbled by this power encounter. And in his humility he reached out by saying, "Lord, what would You have me to do?"

From the moment that the flame of God touched Paul, he was forever a changed man. His name changed, his purpose changed, and the direction of his life changed. He was no longer known as the persecutor of believers. Instead, from that day forward, Paul was *"a bondservant of Jesus Christ, called to be an apostle, separated to the gospel of God..."* (Romans 1:1 NKJ).

Often, churches and ministers know that their church is no way near where it needs to be, and revival is so far from their vocabulary. They know that they are lost, and they don't have a clue where to begin. The chasm between apathy and revival seems impossible to cross for most churches, and subsequently, it is easier to keep *the machine* of church life and denominationalism going strong.

A humble believer can easily evaluate the fruit of his life and determine its value. A humble believer can easily decide to make the necessary changes in order to bear strong Biblical fruit. But, it is easier for a religious person to stick his fingers in his ears to block out the sound of conviction and correction. A religious man is a fig tree that bears no fruit.

Wrong Way or Right Way?

The first time we ministered in South Africa was in 2006. The pastor tossed me the keys to his car, told me that I could use his car for the week and offered me to be free to take it wherever I wanted to go. I am used to the way we drive in America with the steering column, gearshifts, and blinkers positioned on the left side of the car and the wheels on the right side of the road. In South Africa it is completely opposite. Behind the wheel for the first time, my heart began to beat a little harder, and Susie had to help me through the process of unlearning my American style driving.

Finally, I got the car going in the right direction, and we took off down the driveway of the pastor's home. I stepped lightly on the gas, drove into the road when Susie said aloud, "There is a car coming right at us!" I quickly hit the brakes. The driver of the other car was honking his horn and clearly upset with me for almost causing an accident. From that moment, I learned very quickly the correct way to drive in South Africa.

Religious people are the same way. They are stuck spiritually, driving on the wrong side of the road, causing accidents left and right. But the humble man is positioned properly, driving on the correct side of the road, avoiding the religious drivers who are set on owning the road.

Religion does things with a wrong mindset and motives, and it is going the wrong way! Religion may be moving; the direction is traveling, but it is not the correct one.

Jesus preached to the lost and he never had trouble with any of them, but His battle was always with the religious people. Eventually, disagreeing with Jesus wasn't enough; they had to crucify Him. Religion in Christianity is the same today. When confronted with grace and the outpouring of revival, it is not enough to disagree; it shouts, "Crucify." The world has little trouble with the church, but religion is what battles the presence of God. Because *some people may get offended*, religion fights for shorter services. Because *some may get offended,* religion keeps the Holy Spirit out of the meetings. Religion is always running in the wrong direction.

To Change or Not to Change

You can be certain of one thing with revival, it will always reveal the heart of every matter. Revival does not bring offense; it exposes the offense that already existed. Revival does not bring rebellion; it exposes the rebellion that already existed. Revival does not bring division; it exposes the division that already existed. Revival is transparent; it hides nothing. In revival we are exposed and vulnerable. Our innocence is restored and godly wisdom, plentiful.

And the one constant in revival is change. When something is old to you, then it is no longer real to you; and raw revival is so real that it causes everything to grow and change, and flourish and blossom.

Paul was hungry for change. Likewise, with all of our hearts, we need to cry out for long-lasting change in the way we have been doing things. We need to cry out like Moses, "Lord, show me your ways." As we open ourselves to change, it is then and only then that the spirit of revival can breathe on our religious dead bones.

The Spirit of God is looking for a reason to pour out His presence upon every church and every person. However, at the same time, there are no short cuts to revival in your church and in your life. Unless there is a continual willingness to change and be more transformed, there will be no long-lasting revival. When a person is a young Christian, they are open for change. It's like the presence of God hovers over and around them because of their child-like heart for change and their sincere hunger for more of God's power.

True historical and Biblical revival does not come to people based on their conditions. Instead, true revival is based on the heart condition for change and hunger for the power of God.

The truth is, the sun will always rise in the east and set in the west. The truth is, what goes up must come down. The truth is, a desire and willingness to change is essential to revival in your life and ministry.

CHAPTER 4
CONNECTING AND DISCONNECTING OF REVIVAL

A few years ago, I decided to bring home a new puppy as a gift to my wife. With his coal black eyes, floppy ears, and unconditional love, he quickly made his way into our hearts and our family. As puppies can be adorable, they also are capable of being very naughty. We wanted to train him while he was still a puppy, and we signed him up for the Puppy Training Course at our local pet store. We all learned a lot from our two-week course. Our puppy learned to obey our commands, and we learned that dogs have the amazing ability to separate from their past and "live in the now."

"Living in the now" or *disconnecting and reconnecting* is a key principle of revival and to living in the Kingdom of God. The Holy Spirit revealed this principle to me, many years ago, and it has been revolutionary to my life, and I have been sharing it around the world ever since.

With every step of our Christian life, we must continually make the decision to either let go of the past and move into our inheritance in God, or remain living our life from the past. Your past may be full of hurt, disappointment, and failures, or perhaps your past was simply a lukewarm Christian lifestyle. Either way, in order to connect with revival, we must disconnect with the good and the bad of the past. Just as in the case of our furry family friend, we must learn to live for today, focusing all our efforts and energies on what lay before us. We must learn to disconnect from the voices and temptations of our past, leaving behind the darkness that holds us back spiritually, and step into the light.

I remember ministering to a gentleman during a church meeting. He confessed that he still had a stash of marijuana hidden in his home. He kept it *just in case* he could not keep clean. Of course, he was still smoking it and addicted to it for years, but in his mind, he wanted it there just in case. That was his voice of temptation from his past with which he was still connected. If we do not cut the cord to our past, then it does not matter what may happen to us in the altar. We will find ourselves going back into the old habits and patterns that we thought we had received freedom.

Is God Finished with Revival?

Cutting the cords of old habits is just as essential as cutting cords to the old wine of religion. By leaving open a way to go back into dead, lifeless religion, slowly we will lose the passionate hunger for revival fire in our heart.

In 1996, a Charismatic periodical reported that some 2,000 revivals were currently burning all over North America. But by January of 1997, there were less than fifty still burning. Was God finished? The answer is a resounding NO! The reason so many of these revival fires burned out so quickly is that they found the cost too rich a price. Church life could be made much easier by going back to the old religious programs and schedules. Church as usual didn't offend "Mr. Big Bucks" or the head intercessor of the church. One pastor told me that the reason they decided not to continue pursuing revival fire is that the people in his church were tired; they weren't used to going to church three days a week. Instead, he said they preferred to go back to once a week church on Sunday mornings.

"For which of you, intending to build a tower, does not sit down first and count the cost, whether he has enough to finish it—lest, after he has laid the foundation, and is not able to finish, all who see it begin to mock him, saying, 'This man began to build and was not able to finish'" (Luke 14:28-30 NKJV)?

Many people want to enjoy the benefits of revival without giving into the cost of revival. They want the crowds to pour into their church, the notoriety and recognition; they even don't mind the extra money, but many of those same people do not count the full expenditure of revival. The cost may mean giving up "me time."

Maybe the cost of revival means giving up your family vacation to host the presence of God. Maybe it will cost you your reputation; after all, what will the other churches in your area, or your denomination, think of you?

Revival is meant to be more than just an ankle-deep manifestation of the giggles, or a few tears running down your face. Those manifestations are wonderful and we believe in them; however, they are the by-product, the side-dishes, not the main course of revival. Revival means change is coming and it is imminent; if you will allow the change to come, then revival will find a landing pad in your heart, life, and church.

Let the River Get in You

Revival demands change. All too often, people only have a shallow depth of revival fire in their hearts and life. The reason is simple; we don't yet realize that God's goal is change in the life of the church, individual, or city. If we do not allow our heart attitudes or motives to be challenged, then how will the revival fire continue to burn? You must have a willing heart to let God expose you, challenge you, and even bring humility to you. Not that He will humiliate you, but instead, He wants you to humble yourself according to the book of James, so that in time He can lift you up.

John G. Lake was a great revivalist in the early 1900s. In the life of his ministry, he raised many people in miracles. He told of a time when he was ministering in a remote village in South Africa. As he arrived to the village, he was told that two people drowned and had been dead for hours. It was a mother and her daughter. The daughter was swimming near the riverbank when she began to drown. The mother was screaming for help, but no one could reach her daughter. The mother jumped in to save her daughter, but the river overcame both the mother and her daughter and they perished.

The people were weeping as they retrieved the bodies from the river when John G. Lake approached the horrific scene. Lake went right into the midst of the chaos and weeping, and he bent down over the bodies that had been dead for hours. Then, he spoke to them the words of life.

Within seconds after he spoke the words of life, both the mother and her daughter came back to life, and were both raised from the dead. When mother and the daughter were raised up, Lake said to the crowd, "The difference between mother and daughter and the rest of you is simple, you all were *in* the river, but they were the only ones to allow the river to get *into* them!"

"For the word of God is living and powerful, and sharper than any two-edged sword, piercing even to the division of soul and spirit, and of joints and marrow, and is a discerner of the thoughts and intents of the heart" (Hebrews 4:12 NKJV).

The Word of God is a piercing sword and discerner of the thoughts and intents of the heart. We must allow the knife of God's power to transform us into the very image of the Christ. We must allow it to cut out things not like Him in our heart. Many believers have habits and attitudes that are unlike Christ, but by His grace and power, those attitudes and habits can be burned out by the fire of God.

Is Your Comfort the Ultimate Goal?

"Do not think that I came to bring peace on earth. I did not come to bring peace but a sword. For I have come to 'set a man against his father, a daughter against her mother, and a daughter-in-law against her mother-in-law'; and 'a man's enemies will be those of his own household.' He who loves father or mother more than Me is not worthy of Me. And he who loves son or daughter more than Me is not worthy of Me. And he who does not take his cross and follow after Me is not worthy of Me. He who finds his life will lose it, and he who loses his life for My sake will find it" (Matthew 10:34-39 NKJV).

Some years ago, these words of Jesus in Matthew became alive to me, *"Do not think that I came to bring peace on earth. I did not come to bring peace but a sword. For I have come to set a man against..."* The revelation of these words came when I realized that Jesus was not calling for a literal war. Instead, Jesus was calling for a confrontation to the Pharisaical mentality that can so easily live in Christian believers. In the context of what Jesus is speaking of here, the war is not in the heavens; the war is in the mindset of hardhearted people who refuse to change.

When we give our heart and life to Jesus, we are to die to self and choose to do His will. That means we die to our goal of comfort and obey God to bring in the harvest—even if it makes us uncomfortable. The ministry of Jesus was not one of comfort. Imagine His mother, Mary. Her purpose in this life was to give birth to the savior of the world, the Son of God. Think of the conversation she must have had with her father—pregnant, not married. I'm sure Mary was uncomfortable with the rumors that followed her as she and Joseph raised young Jesus. And yet, she accomplished her life purpose.

In other words, yes, God is the great Comforter, but His goal is not to make you comfortable all the time. He will take you out of the comfort zone to use you for His glory, but you must be willing. His goal is worldwide revival fire, whether or not it's convenient or comfortable for you. To be a part of His ultimate plan takes our total surrender to do His will. Our comfort does not equate with God's will in our lives.

I have heard believers speak unscriptural statements such as, "Well if it's difficult, then it must not be the Lord." Or, "If God doesn't open a door, He will open a window." While that sounds great to our flesh, I am sure the Apostle Paul, along with most the other saints from the New Testament, would boldly disagree. When Paul received instruction from the Holy Spirit to go to a foreign land, if he had to, he broke down the doors set up by men who opposed the will of God. As a result, Paul's comfort was often times non-existent.

"From the Jews five times I received forty stripes minus one. Three times I was beaten with rods; once I was stoned; three times I was shipwrecked; a night and a day I have been in the deep; in journeys often, in perils of waters, in perils of robbers, in perils of my own countrymen, in perils of the Gentiles, in perils in the city, in perils in the wilderness, in

31

perils in the sea, in perils among false brethren; in weariness and toil, in sleeplessness often, in hunger and thirst, in fastings often, in cold and nakedness—besides the other things, what comes upon me daily: my deep concern for all the churches" (II Corinthians 11:24-28 NKJ).

When revival comes knocking at our door, we must silence the Pharisee within that screams out, reminding us of all the comforts we may not receive. We must do what is necessary to silence every voice of distraction, even when it comes through loved ones, our pastors, and even people we have known and trusted for years. We need to stand for revival and shout the Word of God to every doubting, divisive voice, *"Get behind Me, Satan! For you are not mindful of the things of God, but the things of men"* (Mark 8:33 NKJV).

"Don't You Dare Touch My Doctrines!"

The transforming fire of Heaven came to many different groups over the last two-thousand years, and every time, there was a reformation, especially in the area of their doctrines. When Martin Luther came onto the scene some five-hundred years ago, he came with a message of radical grace, and those who held the power within the Catholic Church fought with a vengeance to stop the message of grace forever. Because Luther challenged the Pharisaical false doctrines of the Catholic Church, a death sentence was issued on his life, forcing him to flee into hiding at Wittenberg Castle in Germany, just to keep from being killed from the minions of the Catholic Church. There, he successfully translated the Latin Bible into the modern day language, allowing the masses to read from the Holy book for themselves for the first time in history.

In 1901, when Charles Parham and his Topeka Bible school students began to preach and teach about the baptism of the Holy Spirit and speaking in tongues, people would line the streets of the city and throw rotten tomatoes and eggs at these holy saints as they passed by. In France during the 1400s, a teenage girl, named Joan of Arc, declared that Jesus had appeared to her. She told the religious leaders about her experiences with supernatural visions and how in

32

these visions she felt called by God to save her beloved France. This illiterate, peasant, teen-aged girl lead the army of France against the tyranny of England and succeeded in her mission. But because she challenged the religious doctrinal status-quo of her day, many of the religious people wanted her dead. They succeeded in their mission, and she was burned at the stake when she was just 19 years old.

In Mark chapter 1, Jesus approached brothers, Peter and Andrew, as they were fishing with their father, Zebedee. Notice that Jesus did not ask the men, "Is this a good time for you to leave your father and the family business to come follow after me?" He did not say, "As soon as you have six confirmations, seven prophetic words, and the approval from your pastor, then, only if you want to, come follow me."

Jesus gave a command as they were in the middle of life, as usual, mending fishing nets. The Bibles says that immediately they followed Him. They didn't hesitate. They dropped the family business, salary, and retirement plan, to follow the Master. This seems to me like they knew how to disconnect from the voice of human reason and logic, doubt and fear, and reconnect with the voice of God.

It has happened many times throughout my Christian life that I had to make a choice to yield to the wind of change. When confronted with Truth, I have willingly killed the Pharisee in my mind and changed my doctrines in order to grow in the things of God. I have learned that when the Master calls, that is the time that I immediately and eagerly drop my nets and follow Him.

Too many times, I have witnessed man's refusal to move, change, and adjust, in order to accommodate the desires of God. Stiff-necked people stop the anointing outpouring of God's presence and power, and that is when the fire of revival wanes, and man goes back to worshiping his *golden calf* religion.

God loves to mess up our religious patterns and confound the wisdom of the wise with the foolishness of God. God wants to form His Church into a new group destined for the purpose of revival. We must be willing! We must be prepared! We must disconnect from the old and reconnect with the Spirit of God.

CHAPTER 5
HEARTFELT REVIVAL WORSHIP

"Oh come, let us worship and bow down; Let us kneel before the Lord our Maker. For He is our God, And we are the people of His pasture, And the sheep of His hand" (Psalms 95:6-7 KJV).

The best tool for propelling any revival is heartfelt revival worship. It is the kind of worship that God responds to and loves. Heartfelt revival worship takes place when you worship God with hunger and mean it with all your heart. It is a journey, an experience, a dance. Heartfelt revival worship happens as we bow our hearts motives and consciously surrendering everything to Him—it's allowing Him to become the Guest of Honor, the center of it all.

In August of 1982, I was a young teenager. I was born again through a small youth group in my town. Soon after my salvation, the youth group encouraged me to join them at a large church meeting located about a hundred miles away, and I made the journey. I had been listening to the group leader tell us about being filled with the Holy Spirit and about speaking in other tongues. If it was God, then I was excited to have it. All of my friends were having wonderful Holy Spirit encounters, and I had such a hunger to receive the infilling of the Holy Spirit too.

With each mile we drove, the hunger in my heart grew stronger. I could hardly contain my joy. I told the Lord that I was going to receive the infilling of the Spirit that night and that I would be the first to get it. It was a cold January evening when we arrived at the church. The worship had already begun. We made our way to our seats and as the worship music powerfully built, it became more passionate. I looked around to see my friends raising their hands in worship. Ladies were dancing in the isles of the church. Some of the men were kneeling at the altar. Oh, my heart was longing for what they had received, and I wanted to give to God what they were able to give Him.

The worship music had so prepared my heart that as soon as the church elder announced an altar call for all those who wanted to receive the infilling of the Spirit, I made a mad dash to the front with such a great expectation. I closed my eyes and to my surprise, both my arms shot straight up into the air. In the background, I could hear the worship band still passionately playing. Then the pastor began to share with us about this wonderful baptism in the Holy Spirit, and before he could finish his lesson I erupted in speaking, or rather, shouting, in tongues. All my heart wanted to do was to go back into the meeting, worship some more with the worship team, and pour my heart out to the Lord.

Worship and praise in music is not just another preliminary that must take place before the *MAIN* part of the church service can begin. Instead, worship *IS* the main part. The worship sets the tone for the rest of the service. While we worship, our hearts open up to all that Heaven has waiting for us, in the realm of the Spirit.

April Showers

By 1999, I was living and traveling in the evangelistic ministry out of Tulsa, Oklahoma. I was spending some much needed time at home after I'd been on an extended ministry trip that had taken me from Oklahoma to Canada to California and then back to Oklahoma. I was exhausted and I needed some rest. One night, I was up very late praying. I had gotten so lost in prayer and worship that I lost track of time. By the time I checked the time again, it was almost three o'clock in the morning.

I finally found my way to bed and pulled the sheets and blanket up to me, tucking myself nicely into bed. I closed my eyes and could feel my body and mind drifting asleep. But within moments, I was jolted awake by the audible voice of Almighty God. Although, I had experienced this twice before, I don't believe that it's something I could get used to hearing. I was shocked at what I heard Him say. God had indeed spoken and I was listening.

36

I heard Him say, "Tom, You say, April showers bring May flowers." Then there was silence. I was so alarmed and the fear of God was all over me that I could hardly even get myself to reply. Again, I heard Him say, "Tom, You say, April showers bring May flowers, but I say that it is your FLOWERS of worship that rise and ACEND, that cause the showers of My blessings to come down and DECEND upon you."

In that moment, I realized that the Holy Spirit was speaking to me about my worship. I understood how very important and essential worship is to life and ministry.

Since that experience, my heart is so easily swept away in worship, more than any other time of a church service. I am on a Journey every time I step into a consecrated time of praise and worship. I am there to give to God, and I purpose to give Him my very best every time. Our hearts should melt in worship. In worship, our focus should be fixed on pleasing Him, giving to Him, adoring Him. And, in essence, worship is a time that God gets to hold His children and interact with them.

Throw Your Heart into It

Let me break a myth about worship. Heartfelt revival worship does not need a good voice, a full band, a robed choir, lights, smoke, or even instruments to be heard by the Lord. The only non-negotiable thing that is needed for heartfelt revival worship is, your heart. Something that touches people so deeply is heartfelt worship—when you mean every word that comes out of your mouth. It is the heart totally abandoned to God that touches the Master's heart, and it touches everyone's hearts around you.

Some years ago we were ministering in Ohio, and it was a noticeably *performance driven* church. A little before the service, Susie and I were in the back room fellowshipping with the pastor. He turned to us and said, "We're going to just hang out here in my office until the worship is just about over, and then we'll make our grand entrance. That's how the big guys do it." We were so grieved, as these words seemed to linger in the air above our heads. Without another moment of hesitation and with the sincerest gracefulness

Susie replied, "Pastor, I truly prefer to be small in my own eyes, and, if it's alright with you, I would like to join in the worship service. Next to my husband's preaching, the worship is my favorite part of every service. Besides, that's where God really seems to like talking to me." Needless to say, the pastor was a bit stunned and a little offended, but he kindly pardoned us to join the worship, and it was one of the most amazing times in worship we had in the history of our ministry. It was our desire to worship the Lord that night. We were not there to entertain people or be the big shots for the evening. We were there to bring the fire of God and set the captives free, and we knew that in order to do that, we needed to start with passionate honor toward God.

I know that many large churches and evangelists love to have a grand entrance with all eyes on them, when the worship is just about over. I've never subscribed to this way of thinking. With their actions, it is as if they were telling the people, "Worship is for you people; we ministers don't need it because we've got it all." Some ministers have told me that they need that time before the service to "Pray and prepare in the Spirit." What? The worship service isn't the time or place for preparation. Preparation should have been done long before. Worship is the time when we give to God, show honor for God, and corporately connect with the Spirit of God. Many, many times I've had the Holy Spirit completely change my message during the worship, despite what I had already prepared.

Everyone, especially the church ushers, were shocked as we entered the sanctuary to join in worship with the congregation. We learned later that the people had never seen a guest minister enjoy the presence of God in worship like we did. We jumped when the people jumped; we danced when the people danced. Then when the deep worship started, the Holy Spirit moved me to kneel before Him. This is a very normal thing for me during worship, so like many times before, I knelt before the Lord. When I did, a spirit of humility and hunger swept through the building like a thunderous storm. People everywhere began to fall to their knees in worship. One young man, who looked to be about sixteen years of age, ran to the front of the sanctuary, threw himself to his knees and raised his hands to the Lord. He looked up to heaven, smiling and weeping at the same time. It was as if he knew that his offering was pleasing to God.

Upon seeing the display of passion and honor from that young man, the senior pastor began to weep heavily, and he too, fell on his face in the altar before the Lord. As the tears fell from his face, you could actually see the years of arrogance and self-worship fall from his heart to the carpet. A right and humble spirit had been restored in his heart, right then and there. His wife later confessed to us that she had never seen her husband respond with emotion in church before that night.

We have remained good friends with this pastor and I am blessed to tell you that, to his own admission, not a worship service goes by that he doesn't set the example and passionately engage in the presence of God.

Pass the Rocket Fuel Please

Worship will always be the fuel of any revival. In Florida, we live close to Cape Canaveral, where many rocket ships and space shuttles take off for their outer space missions. I have always been fascinated with space, so one summer, I decided to take my family to visit the space station and explore Cape Canaveral. As we toured the spacious buildings, we learned about how the NASA team actually launches the space rockets.

Before a rocket is ready for launch, it takes hours to fill the mammoth device for its departure with enough fuel. As they pour in the liquid rocket fuel, it is explosive and very volatile because of the power that it contains to propel the space ship to its proper destination. As our guide was explaining this to us, I couldn't help but see the similarities to worship. As rocket fuel is to the rocket ship, so is worship to revival. Our worship contains the very powerful and explosive fuel that it takes to thrust revival to its proper destination and destiny.

For years, Susie and I were a part of a major revival in the middle of the United States. Often times, right before worship was to begin, the worship leader would remind us all, "As you sing tonight, make every word count, and mean everything that you say and sing to the Lord; worship is a journey and it has a destination, and together we're going on that journey tonight." He would instruct us and remind us often that this was the time of purpose and destiny, not a time to lifelessly mutter out the words on the overhead.

All too often, we want the worship leader to bring us into the presence of God or we want to rely on a song to take us there. Worship is personal. No one can do it for you. Worship is a personal engagement of one's heart to God's—sometimes done corporately and sometimes alone—but it is always personal. You must do the singing, you must do the dancing, you must do the kneeling, you must raise your hands, and you must shout to the Lord. A worship leader should be there only to help lead you to the destination. You must go on the journey; no one can worship God for you.

Outward Expression
of Inward Passion

Keith is a close friend of mine who stands over six-feet tall, and has a voice that booms like thunder. Most people's reaction to his body size is immediate intimidation. There are many dimensions to this man, and he's a great friend to have around, especially when you need a little muscle to back you up. Years ago when I was first getting to know him, he said to me, "I'm just not an emotional guy." I took him at his word. At least, I took him at his word until I watched the Superbowl with him later that year. Let me tell you, he was highly emotional from start to finish. He was an emotional guy after all—it was just a matter of finding his passion.

Like Keith, many in the church excuse their lack of interest in church and in revival as, "I'm just not an emotional or expressive person." And, like Keith, I would believe them until someone speaks derogatory about their political party, or their favorite sports team, and so on. Touch on their passion and their emotions will run wild. These normally timid people become angry or excited, they begin screaming or cheering, and suddenly, they are very outwardly demonstrative. Sadly, many in the church have emotions and passion for other things, but none for Jesus Christ.

Your internal heart will always follow your external expression. If you are weary and tired from a long week, you will be shocked at how much energy you will begin to have once you give God your very best during the worship service.

Often, giving your best means demonstrating on the outside what is happening on the inside. I have never seen a person who is passionate about a thing and then lifelessly sit to the side and unemotionally observe.

I can remember an experience I had during a worship service some years ago. I was so lost in the presence of God that night. My eyes were closed, my voice was loud, and my hands were raised. I was so full of the passion of God, and I deeply and desperately wanted to outwardly demonstrate my love for God more and more. I tried to raise my arms higher and higher and higher. I wanted to reach heaven with my hands. As I stood there reaching as high as my body would allow, I suddenly felt the hands of the Holy Spirit take my hands. He physically took my hands into His. I will never forget what it felt like the night the Holy Spirit took hold of my outstretched hands.

Worship is not singing songs. It is much, much more than that. Worship is not singing slow songs. Worship is the souls desire and it is the hearts attitude. Worship is something that each person must do for themselves, and the only one who can see it, is God. It may be easy to con the church members around you, your family, your pastor, the board members, your spouse, but you cannot con the Holy Spirit. If you will give your best in worshiping God, you will be engulfed with God's presence, and revival fire will burn strong in your heart.

Which Way Are We Singing?

I have enjoyed many worship services. Each one is unique and each one is special in some way because I choose to make the best of every worship service, regardless of the talent or circumstances.

Worship songs can be man-to-man, or horizontal, in their message. They are good, but the anointing on these songs are usually minimal. Horizontal worship songs are not directly sung *to* God. These songs have lyrics directed *to* man, *from* man, and are usually, but not always, *about* God. While these songs are typically not life-changing, heart-wrenching songs, they can be used to encourage ourselves and each other along in our Christian journey. However, when the worship lyrics turn vertical, man-to-God, then the river of God will explode with great power and presence.

Vertical worship starts on earth and reaches up to heaven. Vertical worship is the most powerful and impacting because we are singing *to* God and *about* God. He is the focus of our gaze, He is the focus of our words, and His presence is worth our full attention and our full adoration.

We were invited to minister at a church in the mid-western part of the United States. The pastor and the worship leader had together grown very hungry for revival, and they wondered what they could do to stir up revival among the people in the church. I asked them if I could attend the Sunday morning service without ministering, for the purpose of observing. How would I be able to help set them in the right direction if I didn't know which way they needed to be turned?

That Sunday morning we attended. Many of their songs were horizontal worship. In fact, most everything, including the announcements, the offering, and the preaching, were all horizontally focused.

That night, I was set to preach. I was introduced after the worship ended and I made my way to the front of the church. I leaned over to the worship leader and asked him if I could please use his guitar. With his permission, I took the guitar and with all my heart, I started to play a deep, passionate, vertical worship song to the Lord.

I closed my eyes. I played and sang my heart out to God.

"This is the air I breathe.
This is the air I breathe.
Your holy presence,
Living in me.
You are my daily bread.

You are my daily bread.
Your very Word,
Spoken to me.

And I, I'm desperate for You.
And I, I'm lost without You."

© 1995 Vineyard Mercy Publishing
Words and Music by Marie Barnett

As I played and sang this song, something changed in that church that Sunday night. The sweet spirit of reviving fire lit the hearts of the people with fresh passion and love for Jesus. The people of the congregation joined me and together we worshiped God deeply. The glory of God swept into that sanctuary and nothing else seemed to matter. For the first time in a long time, the subject was not about the church, the pastor, the song, the offering, the children's ministry, or the youth car wash. It was all about Jesus—only Jesus.

Open Your Heart
And Go For It

Open your heart and become vulnerable to the Holy Spirit in worship. Allow Him to touch you, and speak to you during this wonderful time. As you magnify the Lord, you change the focus from your problems onto your Heavenly Father. As you open your heart and worship the Lord, everything will change—even your perspective. The deepest, most powerful experiences can easily be had during heartfelt revival worship. These are the times when you will see the phenomenal outpouring of God's Spirit intensify in your life and take you to the places that you've longed for in the Spirit.

CHAPTER 6
CHILDREN AND YOUTH IN REVIVAL

"Train up a child in the way he should go, And when he is old he will not depart from it" (Proverbs 22:6 NKJV).

One of the wonderful traits of revival is that it is not a respecter of persons. It does not choose an age group, a gender, a certain skin color, or a specific geographical location. Revival can invade anyone, anywhere, no matter their station, social or economic status, or the generation in which they were born.

Children, youth and young adults have played critical roles in revivals throughout history. A great example took place in Wales during the Welch Revival of 1904. The revival that shook all of Wales started when a young evangelist, Evan Roberts, ministered at in a youth meeting. That night sparked a revival that within one year found the entire country of Wales burning with revivals fire. During the life of the Welch Revival history tells us that as the glory of God would fall like the rain, the children would be the first ones in the altars, and the last ones to leave the services.

In the 1700's when the flames of revival took over the north east coast of the United States of America, it was the children that were swept up, and chiding the adults to get hungry and put away the childish and foolish things of the flesh.

During this time, there was a young six-year old boy who was attending public school. One day, the boy asked permission from his teacher if he could please be excused to use the outhouse. The outhouse was located behind the small wooden school house. Permission was granted and the boy made his way out of the school building and around the back to the outhouse. About ten minutes had passed and his teacher noticed that the boy hadn't returned to class. She asked the boy's older sister to go check on the boy. She told her to go and make sure he wasn't playing outside and bring him back to class. Another ten minutes goes by and the teacher notices that neither the boy, nor his sister had returned to class.

A bit frustrated, the teacher decides to send out one of the older students to get them both and bring them back to class. So, the older teenager did as she was instructed, but she too was gone for ten minutes. Upset, the teacher walked outside to see, for herself, what was going on with the three students that had left. There behind the school building were all three children kneeling on the ground next to the outhouse, crying out to God for revival to come to the school house. Upon hearing their cries to God, the teacher walked over to the children. The young boy stopped praying, looked at his teacher and spoke prophetically, "Ma'am, I am sorry, but we must be about the Master's business, and His business is revival in this town."

Coloring Books or The Holy Ghost?

Secular humanism suggests that good parenting is demonstrated by allowing the child to experiment on its own. Furthermore, it suggests that through his or her own experimentations, each child can then decide, for himself, what is right and what is wrong. But Proverbs 22:6 instructs us to, *"...TRAIN up a child in the way he should go..."*

Any horse trainer, who is worth their weight, will tell you that a common method used to train horses is to yoke, or tie, the younger horse with the stronger horse. This way the younger horse will be *trained* in the way they should go. Contrary to modern-day parenting techniques, God built within man the need and the desire to be taught, or trained. Just like the young horse, our children need to have the example set for them, and they must learn what is the right way and what is the wrong way.

Children must be trained in the area of worship. Many churches have a separate room where the children can go and be entertained during the service, instead of using this time to train and teach children how to worship. On the other hand, if the children join their parents in the sanctuary, they are usually given coloring books and crayons, video games and books to keep them occupied, instead of helping them to engage in the Holy Spirit happenings of the service.

As I mentioned before, Susie and I have been in many major revivals, and some not as well-known revivals around the world. One of the things that transformed my thinking, in this area, was when we attended the *Smithton Outpouring* in Smithton, Missouri. Learning from history, this group placed priority on their children.

Never before had I seen children trained how to seek the presence of God, crying out in one accord, lifting their hands in the front of the worship service—and loving every moment. Their passion, intensity, and pureness of heart made me weep many times. I watched their teachers encourage them to give God their very best. Their teachers and parents showed them what giving God their strength really looked like.

Mayday! Mayday!

When parents provide their children with a constant diet of entertainment, they grow up with a skewed view of what this life, and a life spent living for Jesus Christ, is about. Likewise, when children and youth have had no grace-filled discipline and have been given only weak examples in the Kingdom of God, they will naturally be bored, and in their mind, church becomes dull, along with God's Kingdom. Of course, they will not want to be in church—they've never been given the appetite for the things of God's Kingdom.

For the sake of busyness, career, technology, and so on, the modern parent is consciously or subconsciously, training their children that from the moment they wake up they must be entertained. Our children go to school and have more entertainment. When they return home, they are exposed to an even greater sea of entertainment—until they fall asleep with an iPod turned on and the television playing in the background. This constant diet of entertainment will affect the way they think and react to the things of God. In addition to that, it will affect the way they think and react to God, Himself.

There is a crisis happening in most churches. Sadly, when you look over most congregations, there is a sea of gray heads. While it blesses me to see the faithful saint attending church, it also alarms me that without a focus on the young people, most churches will likely shut their doors in fifteen years. This is because most churches focus on the 40 year old and older crowd. We must have revival in our churches. We must allow revival to reset our path. The church of Jesus Christ, today, must place a strong emphasis on our young people. They are the church of tomorrow.

In the natural, imagine a parent who feeds their children a constant diet of cake, cookies, candy and soda. With this pattern of eating, think of what would happen if a plate of meat and fresh salad with vegetables were placed on the table. Well, after years of eating only junk food, it's no surprise that they would reject the nutritious foods, because for years they've not developed a hunger or appetite for the things that are healthy and right.

Church leaders, teachers, parents, and grandparents, we must train our children from infancy how to develop a hunger and thirst for the things of God. Giving your children a coloring book and crayons during church services has not done the job. The revelation must begin in us—that our children are not born with a *junior spirit*. They are given the same Holy Spirit as adults. Their human spirit hungers, and must be developed—just like adults. The same measure of power, the same measure of strength and ability has been given to them, by and through the Holy Spirit.

Teens and Their Issues

During my time in the pastoral ministry, I was a youth pastor in New Jersey and also in California. As a youth pastor, I learned a lot about young people, and I learned even more about the parents of young people. Week after week, I watched hardhearted, disinterested young people dragged into church and youth group by their parents. Often times, the parents would come to me with the hammer of guilt and say, "My kids are so disinterested in God. You're the youth pastor, do something with them!" I felt like saying to them, "You screwed them up for sixteen years, and NOW you want me to fix it in one hour a week?"

During my time as youth pastor in California, there was a couple in the church who were a part of the church leadership. She was the head Sunday school superintendent, and he sat on the church Board of Directors. They had two children, and both refused to come to youth group each week. One day, this couple approached me and pleaded with me to call their children, and take them to lunch. With heavy pressure tactics, they instructed me that it was my duty to persuade their children to attend church and youth group.

Being young in the ministry, I reluctantly did as they asked. One by one, both children said nearly the same thing to me, "I'm not stupid. I know what you're doing and I know my parents made you take me to lunch. My parents are hypocrites and so are most adults. I don't want to go to church and at least I'm honest about who I am." Sitting across the table from them that day, listening to what they had to say, I physically began to feel sick. It was as though my heart was shattered into a million pieces. I was beginning to realize the condition of the church and the even more desperate condition of its youth.

I was born again in my youth. I was only sixteen years old when I prayed a simple, but heartfelt prayer of salvation. Soon after that, I was introduced to the baptism in the Holy Spirit and I spoke in tongues. After I made the decision to serve Jesus, nothing could stop me. Everything in my life was new, and I felt God for the first time. It was impossible for me to be lukewarm or cold toward godly things. It wasn't uncommon for me to lay hands on the Evangelical kids in my high school for them to receive the Baptism of the Holy Spirit. I was so excited about being a Christian that if I found someone sick, I would immediately minister healing.

I had purposefully shut off every other distraction in my life, and this thing inside of me was like an unstoppable force. My parents didn't do it for me, but I chose to change my appetite, spiritually speaking. The more I fed it from the Bible or from Christian books, tapes, and sermons, the more the fire inside of me grew. I was even challenged by my parent's Lutheran pastor, toe to toe, scripturally during a sit down meeting they arranged, hoping to bring me back to my "normal" senses. But this Lutheran pastor's efforts were futile, and it was too late for me. I had already tasted. I had already seen that the Lord was good and I wanted as much of Him as I could take. The fire of God had taken over my heart and life to such a degree, and there was nothing to go back to.

Where to Start?

I think that the best place to start is the place of honesty. We need to stop, evaluate, and honestly question our job of training our children. This must be done individually as parents, and it also must be done corporately as we evaluate the condition of the youth in the church, as a whole. Without condemnation, how would you rate yourself as a trainer of your children in spiritual matters? Are you able to rank yourself high, or would you have to admit to some failures? No matter your answer, there is always another day ahead of us. It is never too late to start over and begin again, if needed. God's grace is more than sufficient. In fact, just as His mercy is new every morning, so His grace is forever available to you.

Cultivating a fresh and new spiritual hunger and thirst in your children is the next step. Reading the Bible daily and praying with your children is so very important. You may have to start slowly— maybe even for ten minutes each day. But as you establish this practice in your home and in your daily life, you will begin to develop something that will take root in their hearts and minds and will remain in their spirit for a lifetime to come.

Starting at home is critical, but training them in the church is just as important. No matter what age, you can begin to patiently train them the importance of raising their voice in song to God. By example, you are able to demonstrate by raising your hands, dancing before the Lord, kneeling in His presence, and attentively listening to the sermon. Involve your children every step of the way. Train them by example to get involved in church, even when they are weary. Speak to them every day about their relationship with the Holy Spirit. Challenge them and teach them to ask the Holy Spirit to show them how to pray, worship, and to read their Bible on a daily basis.

Consistency is the key, and these baby steps are essential to training our children and young people to grow up to be mighty leaders and the revivalists of the next generation.

"Train up a child in the way he should go, And when he is old he will not depart from it" (Proverbs 22:6 NKJV).

CHAPTER 7
LOOKING OUT!

"... And at that time your people shall be delivered, Every one who is found written in the book. And many of those who sleep in the dust of the earth shall awake, Some to everlasting life, Some to shame and everlasting contempt. Those who are wise shall shine Like the brightness of the firmament, And those who turn many to righteousness Like the stars forever and ever" (Daniel 12:1-3 NKJV).

Revival begins as man reaches out to God *for* rescue. Revival lasts by man reaching out to man, in order *to* rescue. Jesus called every Christian believer to evangelism. We are all called to fulfill the great commission, and that includes bringing the lost to Jesus.

After I was saved as a young teenager in 1982, I knew in my heart that I was commissioned to win souls for Christ, but I had never been taught about how to evangelize. In 1989, now a young adult, I pioneered my first church in Bloomfield, New Jersey. Considering that it was a brand new church. Our finances were not yet established, and I was unable to receive a salary; so during the week, I worked a secular job to support my family and help financially sustain the church. One afternoon, while on my lunch break, I stopped into our local Christian bookstore. Little did I know that the Holy Spirit had a divine encounter waiting for me there that day, and it would change my life and ministry forever.

In the bookstore I hovered over my favorite book section, looking for anything from my favorite author. The store clerk was busy helping someone else and Amy Grant's latest hit was streaming through the speakers overhead. Scanning the bookshelves, I overheard the store clerk sharing Christ with the man at the counter. Then I heard her lead the man by praying the sinner's prayer. I was so excited that I started to pray in tongues, under my breath—in hopes that I could somehow aide this new conversion by my intercession.

As the minutes lingered, the store clerk patiently ministered to the man as he wiped the tears from his face. She encouraged him to get involved in a church and to consider taking part in a discipleship class for new Christians.

I waited for the store clerk to finish speaking to the man and as he walked out of the store, I approached the store clerk. Excitedly, I introduced myself and told her that I was a young pastor of a brand new church just down the road. She introduced herself and told me her name was Rose.

Rose was old enough to be my grandmother, and her passion for Jesus erupted from her very being. She shared with me about the man who had just received Jesus after walking in from the street, because he was curious to see what a Christian bookstore looked like. I rejoiced with her, and together we thanked God for His saving grace.

In between customers, Rose and I talked for over an hour. She told me about her call to witness to everyone she came across. Rose was the leader of evangelism in her 8,000 member church. My mouth dropped open when she told me that she led at least one person to Christ every day, sometimes many more. I was speechless. I so desired to have this passion too. I wanted to learn how to evangelize and how to share my faith and love for God with others.

Without hesitation, Rose obligated herself to be my teacher. In fact, she said, "I want to bring my entire evangelism group to your church and we will train your church how they can win their city to Jesus."

A few weeks later, Rose brought her evangelism team, and in my city they helped us lead two-hundred people to Christ, in a single day. My church grew drastically from all the new salvations we had that day and those to follow.

Rose and I grew closer as she mentored me over the next two years, imparting into me an unstoppable passion for souls.

There are twenty-seven books of the New Testament, and over fifty-five percent of it tells us of the advancement of Christianity all over the world. Evangelism is the heart of the New Testament. With so much emphasis on evangelism given in the New Testament, why has it become such a low priority in most Pentecostal churches?

Why did it take seven years for me to find someone willing to live evangelism, and someone willing to pass their passion for souls onto me? Why is discipleship and *cleaning the fish* given emphasis in churches over catching the fish?

"But the righteousness of faith speaks in this way, "Do not say in your heart, 'Who will ascend into heaven?' " (that is, to bring Christ down from above) or, " 'Who will descend into the abyss?' " (that is, to bring Christ up from the dead). But what does it say? "The word is near you, in your mouth and in your heart" (that is, the word of faith which we preach): that if you confess with your mouth the Lord Jesus and believe in your heart that God has raised Him from the dead, you will be saved. For with the heart one believes unto righteousness, and with the mouth confession is made unto salvation. For the Scripture says, "Whoever believes on Him will not be put to shame." For there is no distinction between Jew and Greek, for the same Lord over all is rich to all who call upon Him. For "whoever calls on the name of the Lord shall be saved." How then shall they call on Him in whom they have not believed? And how shall they believe in Him of whom they have not heard? And how shall they hear without a preacher? And how shall they preach unless they are sent? As it is written: "How beautiful are the feet of those who preach the gospel of peace, Who bring glad tidings of good things" (Romans 10: 6-15 NKJV)!

Doctrinal Garbage

One of the earmarks of our ministry is evangelism. Rose imparted to me a deep desire to win souls. She also imparted to me the deep desire to show others how to do the same. We've made this a practice in our ministry, and we do it as often as we are able.

Week after week, Susie and I travel to different churches and ministries bringing the spirit of revival in nightly outpouring meetings. We stir the people in the evening revival meetings with miracles, and then we encourage them to attend the morning meetings, where often times we teach and train the church in evangelism during the afternoons. It is not surprising that most of the people who attend the daily evangelism trainings have NEVER won a single person to Christ in their entire Christian life.

As we train people in personal evangelism, I am continually shocked at where the opposition to it comes from. It doesn't come from the drug addicts, prostitutes, alcoholics, bars, strip clubs, or gang members. Instead, the opposition comes mostly from church leaders. In fact, we have endured heavy opposition from those we trusted the most, even from our own pastor some years ago.

We heard from a church in the Midwest, and the pastor asked us to come have a week of revival services each night. We agreed and the next week we were there. The night meetings were splendid. We watched as the power of God brought great miracles in the church—something they hadn't seen much in the past. We had arranged with the pastor to do evangelism training in the afternoons, starting the second day of our time there. The glory of God fell as we trained the people and by the dozens, we saw young people saved on the college campus right in town.

The people that we trained in this church came back with testimonies of winning their neighbors to Christ. One after another, the church people witnessed and caught amazing spiritual fish. Some of the individuals they approached admitted that they were once Christians, but had backslidden—they came back to Jesus too.

At the time, we had no knowledge of it, but for over a year, even the pastor's son had been strung out on heavy drugs and alcohol. But during those meetings, he was lit a fire with the glory of God. As the week went on, the church people grew more and more excited for evangelism. The evening meetings were swelling up with all the new visitors, especially the college students who came to check out what was happening at the local community church.

When the meetings had ended, we returned to our offices in Kansas City. That same day, I got a phone call from the pastor of the church. On the phone, he and his wife said that they wanted to talk to me about our approach to personal evangelism. He continued to tell me that despite all of the wonderful testimonies from his church family, he didn't feel comfortable with personal evangelism. He said, "Brother Tom, How can you know with certainty that those people we prayed with are even saved? I believe we gave them false hope of their eternal salvation."

Instantly, I reminded him of Romans 10:9 that says, *"That if you confess with your mouth the Lord Jesus and believe in your heart that God has raised Him from the dead, you will be saved."* As the conversation continued, I could tell that there was no reasoning with the pastor. His mind was made up already, and he was firm on his stand that those precious souls were not really saved.

"Pastor," I said, "I guess I am just foolish enough to simply believe the Bible when it tells me that these people were saved the moment they called on the name of the Lord." Then a boldness like Paul came upon me when the Bible says that he withstood Peter to his face. I said, "Pastor, I don't mean any disrespect, but if I were to follow your logic, then how do I know whether or not you are saved? If praying with someone to receive Jesus wasn't salvation to them, then by what method must a person be born again?"

It is true, only God can see the heart of a man. I wasn't judging the pastor's salvation. Of course, I believed that he was saved. But, the fact is, every person who turned to Jesus that week was also born again. And the doubt and unbelief of the pastor was soon to extinguish evangelism's flame that was now burning strong in the hearts of all the congregants of his church.

The pastor later admitted to me that his interpretation of the Great Commission was to first befriend a person, and then through discipleship class, they would become saved.

Biblically, the emphasis of the Gospels and book of Acts is NOT discipleship—it was evangelism. No matter how you cut it, and no matter how you try to twist it, the fact is that every page put emphasis on evangelism. The great Apostle Paul implored the young Pastor Timothy to *"...do the work of an evangelist ..."* (II Timothy 4:5). Notice that God did not ask him to do the work of a Teacher, an Apostle, a Prophet, or even Pastor—but the work of an evangelist.

They Deserve It

The world deserves to hear the Gospel. They deserve to see it displayed in all its power and glory. They deserve the chance to be set free of sin and sickness. They deserve to hear it from you. Christian television isn't getting the job done. It was never God's great plan to bring salvation to the world just through the medium of Christian television. We, as believers, must proclaim the message to them that provokes them to accept Christ. They deserve to hear the reality of the Gospel of Christ, with all of the benefits that the cross of Christ paid for in their eternal life.

In the Old Testament, God spoke to David about transporting the Ark of the Covenant. God was specific in his instructions to King David, telling him to carry the Ark of the Covenant on shoulders of men. The Ark of the Covenant was a shadow, a representation, of the presence and glory of God.

Rather than follow God's instructions, King David placed the Ark on the new cart drawn by oxen. During the journey, the oxen stumbled. In order to steady the Ark from falling to the ground, Uzza put out his hand. As his hand touched the Ark, he fell to the ground dead. The lesson is that men are supposed to be the transporters of the glory of God, not a man-made cart. We are supposed to carry the message of Jesus' saving grace to the world.

Chances are, you are born-again today because someone carried the glory to you on his or her words and perhaps by their actions. God is not concerned with our natural abilities or inabilities, but He is looking for blind faith and boldness.

From Susie's Heart

Susie writes, "I grew up like most of you reading this book probably grew up—dad, mom, siblings, and Sunday school. I can remember going to church just about as much, if not more than I remember fishing trips, Christmas time, and the occasional playful naughty mischief that would find me in time out or with a well-deserved *swat of correction* on the behind.

Church was always a big part of our family life when I was young. My mother played her role as the children's church superintendent, and my father, the dutiful church deacon, usher, and church leader. At ten years of age during summer camp, I won the award for being the first to zip through my Bible to find the Scriptures, and I never missed bringing my Bible with the blue cover to church each Sunday. But somehow, even in the midst of so much church, I managed to miss Jesus.

By the age of thirteen, my parents had divorced and so many changes had blown in the direction of my family. By this time, my heart was hardening at rapid pace toward church and godly things. The very thought of sitting through another church service seemed less inviting to me than a visit to the dentist.

Two weeks before, I was to turn twenty-one years of age, I found myself up early, driving to work like every typical workday morning. My commute into work usually included a stop at the nearby coffee shop for a hot cup of coffee. Like many days before this day, I bumped into another morning coffee shop regular customer. I knew her only as Jenny, and I estimated that she was probably about my same age.

Unlike me, Jenny was always smiling and full of cheer, despite the early hour. But this morning's coffee stop was different. In fact, it changed my life forever. As we both stood at the counter waiting for our coffee orders, we briefly shared our usual *small talk* about the weather or the score of the previous day's baseball game.

Suddenly, Jenny interrupted by saying, 'Susie, I know I don't know you very well and you don't know me well either. We're both about the same age. We work in the same city. We were both born and raised in the same part of the world. We are a lot the same in many ways.' She continued, 'Really, the only difference between you and I is that I am a Christian and I will live with Jesus forever and you won't.'

I still hadn't fully realized the magnitude of my offense by the time I was able to pick up my jaw off the coffee shop floor. 'Who does she think she is?' I thought to myself. But, before I could gather my thoughts properly in order to form a sentence, her coffee order had arrived, and with a smile and a quick 'goodbye,' she was out the door. I stood there stunned, embarrassed, and honestly ashamed.

With all my strength, I tried to go on about my day and forget those horrible words she had spoken to me at the counter. It seemed that the more I tried to put them out of my mind, the more those words drilled deeper within me. The battle in my mind seemed endless and by the end of the day, they exhausted me. I determined that the next time I saw Jenny, I was going to confront her and teach her a lesson on how inappropriate her exchange had been with me that day. 'After all,' I thought to myself, 'She didn't even know me.'

That night when I returned home after a very long day at work, I could feel the conviction, which felt like torment, heat up even hotter. Now I was alone with only my thoughts. In my mind, I heard Jenny's words over and over again. 'Really, the only difference between you and I is that I am a Christian, and I will live with Jesus forever and you won't.' I did not want to go to hell. I did not really want to go to Heaven either, or at least not right away. But I had to admit to myself that peace was missing in my life. 'Maybe Jesus was the answer after all,' I thought.

The next thing I knew, I was kneeling all alone on the floor of my living room, praying for the first time in a very long time. This time, I meant every word. There were no *thee's* or *thou's* lacing this prayer. I spoke to God as if He were kneeling on the floor in front of me, right there in that room. I said, 'Jesus, If You are real, then I want to know You. Please show me that You are real. If You are all powerful, then I will give You my life. I don't want to live anymore with this hate in my heart. I don't want to live any longer without knowing what this life is all about. If You can show me that, I will do anything and go anywhere You want me to go. All I ask is that You don't send me to Africa or somewhere like that. Amen.'

From that day until today, I've never looked back. I've served every day for Jesus. He has become my closest friend and my deepest ally. I've never backslidden, not for a moment. I've made plenty of mistakes, but I've never felt condemnation from Him, only love, only pure acceptance.

Jenny did not have a Bible degree or theological certificate, but she did have boldness and proven selflessness. Thanks to Jenny, I am a living testimony that Jesus took her simple, yet very straightforward words and changed my world once and forever.

Oh, by the way, one year later, I was serving on the mission field in Tanzania, East Africa. God sure does have a great sense of humor."

Strategies for the Harvest

Truthfully, there are many different ways, forms, and strategies for evangelism. There is *program evangelism*, which is typically one-on-one, personal evangelism. There is *crusade evangelism, servant evangelism,* and *power or prophetic evangelism.*

One of my favorite people in history was a man named, John Wimber. He was known for power evangelism. He even wrote a book titled, *Power Evangelism*. Power evangelism is done by using a demonstration of the power of God, or a Holy Spirit inspired insight into that person's life or circumstances, and at the same of time, presenting the Gospel.

> *"And my language and my message were not set forth in persuasive (enticing and plausible) words of wisdom, but they were in demonstration of the [Holy] Spirit and power (a proof by the Spirit and power of God, operating on me and stirring in the minds of my hearers the most holy emotions and thus persuading them), So that your faith might not rest in the wisdom of men (human philosophy), but in the power of God"* (I Corinthians 2:4-5 AMP).

Ask the Holy Spirit for evangelism strategies that will work for you or your church. As you seek God for wisdom, He will certainly reveal the best evangelism approach for you, and you will be shocked at how much fruit you will reap for the Kingdom. It may not be the most fruitful way to evangelize, but I always encourage people to try *program evangelism*. It will help you to overcome fear of approaching strangers and the fear of rejection. It will also help you gain experience by sharing Christ several times in a short amount of time. While I do use every approach I can think of to evangelize, I personally use *program evangelism* a lot, especially as I travel in airports and busy places that are packed with strangers.

Evangelizing in the Face of Fear

There was a young lady named, Jill, that joined us on one of our annual mission trips. We were headed to Puerto Rico to hold a massive outdoor crusade for a week. During the day, our missions team would hit the streets for a powerful time of evangelism. Jill had never evangelized anyone before. She had been taught that program evangelism was ineffective and intrusive. But, determined to obey God, she got on the airplane.

When we arrived at the San Juan airport, we handed everyone on our team a copy of the mission itinerary that we would be following for the next week. Then we split the large team into several smaller teams, and each team would be strategically placed around the crusade tent each day to evangelize. Nervously, Jill stood in the airport listening to the instructions and literally shaking with fear. Susie noticed her shaking and hoping to help Jill get started; she switched one of her teammates out in exchange for Jill.

The first morning, we met together in a large group for prayer. Then we split up and each team went to their designated area. Some along the beach, some on the streets, and some in the neighborhoods around the crusade area. Susie and Jill, along with the rest of their team, were stationed on the street in front of the crusade area. Taking Jill with her, Susie began to witness to the first group of people she came across. Amazingly, the entire group of young ladies prayed to receive Jesus and they agreed to come to the crusade later that night.

It didn't take Jill long to grow in courage and boldness. Within minutes she had personally won seven people to Christ. Jill broke down right on the street corner, crying like a baby. She had allowed God to use her to share Jesus with these people. She felt so honored and blessed. My group caught up with Susie and Jill's group about an hour later. When she saw us coming toward them, she began jumping up and down on the street corner telling us the stories of all the lost souls she had prayed with that day.

During that trip, God powerfully used Jill, the most fearful one in the beginning. Jill had grown bold and unstoppable. Many were delivered by the power of God as she prayed for them on the street. At the conclusion of the mission trip, Jill had personally evangelized over 320 people. After she would pray with someone on the street, she would write their name in her notebook, so that when she returned home she could continue to pray over them.

What to Pray For

"After these things the Lord appointed seventy others also, and sent them two by two before His face into every city and place where He Himself was about to go. Then He said to them, "The harvest truly is great, but the laborers are few; therefore pray the Lord of the harvest to send out laborers into His harvest" (Luke 10:1-2 NKJV).

Do you not say, 'There are still four months and then comes the harvest'? Behold, I say to you, lift up your eyes and look at the fields, for they are already white for harvest (John 4:35 NKJV)!

I love this teaching from Jesus. He leaves no room for questions. Unlike most church prayer meetings, Jesus didn't tell us to pray for the harvest. The first thing he tells us to pray for are more laborers to go out into the harvesting fields. The fields are ready to be harvested.

When we purposely pray for more workers, two things happen. The first thing is that God begins to answer your prayer for workers and harvesters to come help reap in the harvest. The second thing that occurs is a stirring in your heart to be one of the harvesters sent into His fields.

Another thing that Jesus tells us is to realize the time. The time of the harvest is now. It must not be postponed any longer. The fields are already white for the harvest. In other words, there are no more excuses. I grew up on a farm. I know what the fields look like when the grain is ready to be harvested. I've seen what happens to a field of grain that has not been harvested at the proper time. The soil begins to rot and the entire crop is destroyed.

"Now, Lord, look on their threats, and grant to Your servants that with all boldness they may speak Your word, by stretching out Your hand to heal, and that signs and wonders may be done through the name of Your holy Servant Jesus" (Acts 4:29-30 NKJV).

While attending *Moorhead State University* in Moorhead, Minnesota in 1984, I would wake up every morning for early morning prayer assembly on our campus. As the Christian campus ministry students would come together, we would cry out to God every morning for revival. We would pray that the Holy Spirit would give us fresh opportunities to win our fellow students to Jesus. Our goal was lofty, but we prayed that our entire campus would be born-again and aflame with the Holy Spirit.

We gathered together and prayed with all our hearts. We prayed for what the early church prayed for in Acts chapter 4, boldness. As we prayed for more boldness, I began to notice a change in my character and in my life. I began to fearlessly share Christ with students. I preached the Gospel to the head of the University football team along with anyone else I could. I was learning to live in a new dimension of boldness. Soon, most of the students living on my dorm floor had given their lives to Jesus.

"Praying always with all prayer and supplication in the Spirit, being watchful to this end with all perseverance and supplication for all the saints-- and for me, that utterance may be given to me, that I may open my mouth boldly to make known the mystery of the gospel, for which I am an ambassador in chains; that in it I may speak boldly, as I ought to speak" (Ephesians 6:18-20 NKJV).

Book of Acts at the Supermarket

One of the greatest stories, from our ministry, happened while we were ministering for a month in California. As usual, we scheduled afternoon evangelism trainings, followed by nightly revival outpouring meetings in a local church.

One afternoon, after we had trained the group and prayed over each of them, we took them out to the parking lot of the local Wal-Mart to share Jesus. Susie took one group with her to one end of the parking lot, and I took the other group with me to the other end of the parking lot.

That day, the senior pastor, Alan, joined in and was a part of Susie's team. Pastor Alan was shocked to see just how easy it was to evangelize and share Jesus with people in his own hometown. He watched intently at how Susie would approach the people, regardless of their age or background. He would get so excited that he began to giggle and laugh and then give thanks to God when another person would pray with her.

Pastor Alan was so energized by what was happening that he told Susie, "I'm going to split off from the team and go over to the supermarket just across the street." Susie encouraged him and away he walked with his witnessing tracts and follow-up sheets resting in the front pocket of his short sleeved, button down shirt. He was reviewing the evangelism script that we had provided everyone as he walked across the street and into the parking lot of the supermarket.

The first couple that he saw walking out of the store were angrily arguing with each other. But, Pastor Alan remembered from his training not to pre-qualify people, but to share Christ with everyone. As he approached the couple, he said to them with enthusiasm, "Hi, my name is Alan. I'd like to share two things with you." Never taking his eyes off of the evangelism script, he continued, "God loves you and has a wonderful plan for your life. If you were to die today, would you go to Heaven?"

Shocked, the couple looked at each other and shook their heads, no, with conviction. Pastor Alan kept right with the evangelism script, "Well, the Bible says, 'If you believe with your heart that God raised Jesus from the dead, and if you confess with your mouth that Jesus is Lord, you will be saved.' Now, with tears welling up in their eyes, the husband blurted out, "OK, can we pray with you this confession?" Together, they whole heartily prayed the sinner's prayer with him.

As soon as they said, "Amen" the husband boldly reached into Pastor Alan's front pocket and took out his pen and a follow-up sheet and began to write his name and address on the paper. Pastor Alan was puzzled as to how the man knew he would ask for that information.

Noticing Pastor Alan's bewilderment, the husband turned to the wife and said, "Tell this man of God why I am doing this." The wife told to the pastor, "We have been waiting for you all day long." Pastor Alan said, "I just found out myself that I was coming over here, only minutes ago. How could you be waiting for me all day?" The wife explained, "Because I had a dream last night, and Jesus Christ appeared to me. He told me that someone would tell me all about Him today and show us the way to eternal life today. He said that when I was done talking to the man that we must fill out all the his paperwork."

This encounter sounds like something right out of the pages of the book of Acts. The Holy Spirit had prepared this couple in a dream for what was about to transpire by the power of God.

You might be the answer to someone else's prayer. Just by stepping out in faith you will see the hand of God use you to touch the lost.

If you do not share Christ, who will?

If you do not act in boldness, then who will?

It is time to give away the wonderful grace and mercy that we have received so freely, to all that will receive it.

(You may download free evangelism materials from our website at: www.SHAREtheFIRE.org)

CHAPTER 8
PRAYER AND FASTING

"Now in the church that was at Antioch there were certain prophets and teachers: Barnabas, Simeon who was called Niger, Lucius of Cyrene, Manaen who had been brought up with Herod the tetrarch, and Saul. As they ministered to the Lord and fasted, the Holy Spirit said, "Now separate to Me Barnabas and Saul for the work to which I have called them." Then, having fasted and prayed, and laid hands on them, they sent them away" (Acts 13:1-3 NKJV).

For me, fasting has always been a great delight. Not because I stop eating food for a certain period, but because of all the wonderful benefits I've discovered in fasting. Since I have made fasting a common practice in my life, I have experienced great growth in my spirituality and new depths in my relationship with God. Fasting is a discipline, and there is no doubt that it releases the blessings, anointing, and favor of God in our lives. My wife likes to say that fasting is a quieting of our flesh and an awakening of our spirit.

Many years ago, I gave our entire ministry team a challenge. That challenge was to set one day aside each week and dedicate it to fasting and prayer. For many years, Susie and I had already been fasting almost every Wednesday, and we had seen the benefits far exceed the sacrifice. In fact, there have even been times when our one day fast has lasted for several days and even weeks. And each time, we experience the grace and goodness of God in our lives and ministry anew all the more.

One of the purposes of our weekly corporate fast is for revival. Revival begins in us and we long to live the revival life so that we are able to give the revival life to others. I challenge you to fast and pray for great revival to take place in you, and then in your church and city. It begins with you.

With pure motives, through you, revival is able to transform churches and cities by God's glory. Revival comes to the individual and by sanctifying yourself to God, in fasting and prayer, you will be propelled to a place of increase in miracles, supernatural wonders, and the lost souls softly turning to Jesus.

Benefits of Fasting

"It is written, 'Man shall not live by bread alone, but by every word that proceeds from the mouth of God'" (Matthew 4:4 NKJV).

It may sound like an oxymoron, but fasting begins through our hunger—not our physical hunger, but our spiritual hunger and desire. It produces hunger for God, and it causes your heart to be more sensitive to the voice of God and the realm of the Spirit.

Fasting has amazing spiritual benefits, but it also has great physical benefits also. Fasting gives your body a well-deserved rest. Because our bodies are continually working to digest food and keep you moving, fasting allows our vital organs to reset. It is during these times of fasting that your body is able to purge toxins that have built up in your system for years, flushing them from your body.

One of the physical benefits that I've experienced is that as I fast, my mind becomes clear, crisp, and alert. My mind mends from feeling sluggish and my thoughts are readily sharp. Another physical benefit that I tend to experience almost immediately is a boost in energy and ambition. These are two great physical benefits of fasting.

Fasting the Television

A pastor and his wife were encouraging their entire church to fast the first twenty-one days of the New Year. During their New Year's Eve service they exhorted the people, "We know most of you don't want to fast food, so instead we encourage you to fast the television, video games, movies or the radio during these next three weeks." But, they did not realize that they had reduced the power of God in fasting to a weak Americanized form of consecration. Consecration and fasting are clearly different. I believe that Biblical fasting is fasting food. Whether it be a partial fast, a *Daniel fast,* or a total fast, it is about fasting food.

It is impossible to fast something that is not essential to your life existence. And contrary to what some may think, the television is not essential to our life existence. Fasting is voluntarily doing without food, in order to shut down the sometimes, overwhelming distraction of eating. Silencing the flesh will bring a reviving. When we shut down the distractions, we unlock an even greater sensitivity to God and an even greater presence of God in our lives.

Not Magical

There is nothing magical about fasting. Fasting is as much about prayer as it is about abstaining from food, or certain foods. Fasting is twofold. Without prayer, fasting is only a diet or weight loss tactic. In the Old Testament when God's people were preparing their hearts and lives for what God wanted to do, they always utilized fasting and prayer.

As Brother Kenneth Hagin Sr. used to say, "Fasting changes you." And he was exactly right. Before I had a revelation and understand of fasting and prayer, I used to think that it was a way of getting God to change. No, God does not change. He is absolute and He remains the same through the ages. It is us who must change, and fasting helps to give us strength and humility in which change comes.

Every day we are bombarded with the voice of your flesh crying out for our constant obedience. When our stomach cries out to be fed, we feed it. When our body is weary, we sleep. Our churches are the same, and they are terrified to allow the service to go past the dreaded noon hour on Sunday mornings. Why? Because most people have not disciplined the voice of their flesh.

Three Major Teachings

As we are introduced to the ministry of Jesus in Matthew chapters 5-6, we know that He gave three commands to His disciples and to us, His church. These commands were, "WHEN you give, WHEN you pray, WHEN you fast." These three commands were not suggestions or insinuations. They were absolutes in the life of anyone who followed Jesus, then and now.

Giving has always been central in the message of Jesus Christ. Leading by example, our Father God gave. I am sure that we can all admit that He gave the most costly offering ever given, His only son, Jesus. When God sowed Jesus into this earth, He purposed that His precious seed would yield many sons unto Glory. Like our Father, we too must be givers, especially during times of prayer and fasting.

Prayer is essential to every Christian believer. Prayer comes in many forms and is one of the most powerful tools we've been given by God. Being so essential to the body of Christ, it always amazes me how little focus and priority prayer receives. The biggest threat to an anti-revival religious spirit is connecting simultaneous prayer, fasting, and giving.

Prayer is our lifeline—our direct link to the Creator of all things, and yet most prayer meetings are the least attended. One preacher said, "A church's Sunday morning service tells how popular the church is in the community. The Wednesday night service shows how popular the pastor is to his people. But, the prayer night shows how popular Jesus Christ is in the congregation." That is sad, but true, and only revival can turn that right-side up.

Fasting, to me it seems, is the most challenging for believers of these three commands. The popularity of fasting is weak and admittedly, most Christians have never fasted even a single meal. Some of the reason is that they've not been taught how and why they need to fast, but I don't care what age, gender, or geographical location you are from, fasting is a sacrifice. It only becomes easy and desirable through grace. When we feel the urge or desire to fast, even for one meal, rest assured that the Holy Spirit is preparing you for something ahead.

As we hunger for revival and cry out to God for revival fire to consume us body and soul, then it is essential that we must fast and pray, and we must also give. When we are at the end of religious ritual and routines, and we desire revival more than food or drink to be filled with Jesus, who is the Source of life, He is the Bread that sustains our bodies; He is the New Wine that quenches every thirst. When we hunger for more, we receive more. As we develop an appetite and a discipline for fasting, praying and giving, then God will pour out of His overflow and answer our hunger.

Push Yourself

"Then Jesus, being filled with the Holy Spirit, returned from the Jordan and was led by the Spirit into the wilderness, being tempted for forty days by the devil. And in those days He ate nothing, and afterward, when they had ended, He was hungry" (Luke 4:1-2 NKJV).

One day while working out at the gym, I noticed a man lifting weights in the back corner of the room. He was an average sized man who looked healthy already. He laid down on the bench, situated himself, and firmly gripped the barbell resting on the bar above him. Counting down my own routine, I continued to watch the man. On each end of the barbell he had a very light amount of weight. He bench pressed the weight at least twenty-five times and then positioned himself in a seated position. Clearly, not one bead of sweat could be seen on him. Sarcastically, I thought to myself, "Well, he's never going to be an Arnold Schwarzenegger."

In order to grow a muscle, force must be applied. Resistance in the body challenges the muscle, and they will only grow when they are required to do so. That takes discipline, practice, and heavier weight.

Because our physical lives, often times—if not always, parallel our spiritual lives, it is good practice to allow ourselves to be pushed not to the breaking point necessarily, but pushed toward new growth and spiritual development. I encourage people to pray longer than they are used to and fast more often than they are used to fasting. It's not that we should be like the Pharisees who liked to be seen for their much praying, but because it helps us to keep rule and authority over our flesh. Jesus was never dominated by His flesh—He was always led by the Spirit. He is our supreme example and we must become like Him in every way.

The Fasting Prayer of One

After a meeting one night, I was approached by an elderly lady. She had the look of a seasoned saint and she could have been anyone's grandmother. "Brother Tom," she said, "May I have a moment of your time?" I obliged and invited her to take a seat with me on the row of chairs behind us.

She began to tell me how she had been saved at seven years of age. She was saved after a classmate had invited her to a tent revival that was set up on the outer edge of her small Missouri town. She said, "I've been serving Jesus for seventy-nine years. I have six children, thirteen grandchildren, and five great-grandchildren. Every one of my children, grandchildren and great-grandchildren, who are still alive, are serving Jesus too. Do you want to know why?" "Sure." I said. She continued, "My secret is fasting." When my children were born, I made the decision to fast and pray for them one day a week. When they were old enough, I taught them to fast and pray. Still today, all my children and grandchildren fast with me one day of every week."

After I rejoiced and prayed with her, the senior pastor walked over to us. He said, "Tom, I see you've met my mother." This old gal, along with her late husband, had raised six kids, all of whom are in the full-time ministry—two missionaries, one pastor, an evangelist, a youth leader, and a worship pastor. Most of her grandchildren were also serving in some area of the ministry or in Bible school.

Through her fasting and prayer, she found the key to reaping her families harvest. Fasting brought her and her family into their destinies in God. Because of her obedient, quiet, selfless sacrifice and discipline, all her offspring were aligned in the will of God for their lives.

The Starting Line and The Finish Line

Maybe you have never fasted before or maybe you are an expert at fasting. No matter your experience with fasting, there is always an opportunity to start fresh with new insight and revelation.

If you are waiting to begin your fast until you *feel* like fasting, I guarantee that you will be waiting a long time. No one *feels* like fasting. But by faith you can do it. The Bible says that faith without works is dead. By exercising your faith during a fast, you can avoid the temptations of our flesh. You don't need to have *giant faith* in order to fast. After all, with faith the size of a mustard seed, we are able to throw down the mountains of religion, confusion, pain, temptation, or opposition into the deepest sea.

Jesus told us that nothing is impossible to us because we believe. When I fast, I believe that I will be able to remain faithful and filled with the grace of God to go on. I focus my thoughts on how big God is, not how big my faith is. I stir myself up by reminding myself of how men and women of old fasted and after times of fasting, some of the greatest revivals to ever invade the earth had taken place.

There can be such a tremendous power of faith operating through us, especially as we disconnect from our flesh and connect to the Holy One with our faith though fasting and prayer.

The length of a fast isn't always the most important question. The idea is to start somewhere. Be wise, if you have never fasted before; don't start with forty or twenty-one day fast. Start small and allow yourself time to train your body and mind. Perhaps start by fasting one meal. With God, I've learned that He is not concerned with the longevity of my fasts. He is more interested in raising up men and women who willingly dedicate their lives to seek Him through fasting and prayer. He honors our sacrifices, no matter how small or insignificant we think them to be.

Practicals of Fasting

There is never a "good" time to fast. The best advice I can give is to just start. There will always be an excuse why you shouldn't fast today—family gatherings, holidays, and birthday celebrations. But, I have found that if I just start my time of fasting, the rest of life will fall right into place.

For people who have never fasted or who have never done an extended fast, I always encourage them to start small and build up your faith in this area first. Then when you are ready, a great time to start is at night. For example, start at six o'clock in the evening and then finish the following night at the same time. This technique was a great help to me when I first began routinely fasting.

I encourage people to drink water, and lots of it, during your time of fasting and prayer. There are books available in most Christian book stores that can help educate you on the health benefits of fasting and guide you in the healthiest approaches to fasting.

As you know by now, prayer is as important a part as fasting. Prayer is critical as you fast. It will keep you focused and built-up in your faith. It will open your communication between God, and it will keep you on course during your fast. A good friend of mine told me that when she fasts, she dedicates to prayer and intercession the times during the day that she would normally be eating. I think that is a terrific idea.

Many people have shared with me that the first three days of an extended fast are often times the most difficult. It's been my experience that after the third day, my body kicks into starvation mode and the hunger pangs weaken greatly.

Cotton-mouth and headaches are common effects of fasting, but remember, your body is being cleansed physically and toxins that have built up in your system are being flushed. This can be normal and usually by day three, these effects will subside.

After you finish an extended fast, it is best to ease your body back onto regular foods. Advice from a medical professional or from someone who understands the effects of food and the body, would be great resources.

I'm not a medical professional, but I can tell you by experience that throwing a giant sized bowl of pasta down your gullet after an extended fast is not a good idea. Learning from that mistake, I now acclimate my digestive system slowly by eating soups, raw vegetables, and fresh fruits and salads until my body is back to regularity.

Go For It!

"Blessed are those who hunger and thirst for righteousness, for they shall be filled." (Matthew 5.6 NKJV).

I believe God is already raising you to a new place of hunger and desire in Him. By fasting and praying, He will fill you. This is the hour when "church as usual" doesn't cut it—it just cannot quench that deep longing in God's consecrated people. I challenge you today, fast and pray. When we become hungry we become desperate. And desperate people will do whatever it takes to get a hold of revival, no matter the cost, no matter the sacrifice. Religion and apathy no longer have hold of the hungry heart—their treasure is in heavily places where Christ is seated and we are seated alongside.

I guarantee to you that if you come to God hungry you will leave satisfied. Go ahead, taste and see that the Lord is good.

CHAPTER 9
PASSION,
OUT OF CONTROL

"But I have this against you: that you tolerate the woman Jezebel, who calls herself a prophetess, [claiming to be inspired], and who is teaching and leading astray my servants and beguiling them with practicing sexual vice and eating foods sacrificed to idols." (Revelation 2:20 AMP).

Control is a major hindrance to revival, and passion is a major manifestation of revival. When the Holy Spirit is not controlled by time constraints, or limitations of power displays, then His passion for us becomes overwhelming. Have you ever experienced a moment with the Holy Spirit—perhaps during a powerful worship service, that was so overwhelming, so divine—when His peace and presence were more real than the floor you were standing or kneeling on? If you have, I can guarantee that it took place when the limitations were taken off of God; time was not important, and every distraction became nonexistent.

When the Holy Spirit is allowed the freedom to express His passion, the wake of His demonstration is powerful and life changing. The same is true with Christian believers, revivalists, who are set on a passionate life in the Spirit. Like the Holy Spirit, when believers are limited by the controls of man, false doctrines, and denominations, their passion for the Kingdom of God is stunted and the result is unhealthy, spiritually constipated people.

We most often think of control coming from the devil. We hear people say silly things like, "The devil made me do it." But in reality, it is the control of man that is most common and extremely wicked.

One day a few years ago while sitting in my office, I received a frantic telephone call from Karen, the wife of one of my longtime friends, Bruce, who was the senior pastor at a church in California. I could barely make out what Karen was saying. After she was able to calm down, she told me that Bruce had a massive heart attack that morning and that his doctors were busy preparing him for open heart surgery. I had just talked with Bruce a couple weeks earlier. He told me then that he had been dealing with the usual church politics, and it was beginning to take its toll on him.

Karen explained to me that on the previous night, the Board of Directors called an emergency meeting. After the meeting adjourned, the head board member knocked on the door of the church parsonage, where Bruce, Karen, and their three children lived. He announced to Bruce and Karen that the Board of Directors had just met together and voted Bruce out of his position as the pastor of the church.

In addition, they were asking for Karen's resignation as a teacher in the school. Their reason, she said, was because the majority of the Board of Directors were unhappy that Pastor Bruce was introducing the church to some new things in the Kingdom of God and so, rather than trust that their pastor was hearing from God, they thought it more was appropriate to vote him out.

Upon hearing of the board's decision, they were devastated. Karen's salary from her teaching position in the private school owned by the church, was used to pay for their children's tuition in the private school. As a condition of Bruce's position being the church pastor, their family was given the use of the church parsonage. In one controlling cast of the vote, the Board of Directors stripped my friend and his family of their home, their jobs and income, their ministry, and their children's schooling. It was too much for Bruce's heart to endure, and now his life was hanging in the balance.

Bruce recovered from the massive heart attack, but it took years for he and Karen to recover from the devastation of man's control. Bruce fought hard to rid his heart of hard feelings and bitterness toward the controlling men and women from the board, and he eventually started his own church. Today they are functioning as a very healthy and flourishing local church.

"But to what shall I liken this generation? It is like children sitting in the marketplaces and calling to their companions, and saying: 'We played the flute for you, And you did not dance; We mourned to you, And you did not lament'" (Matthew 11:16-17 NKJV).

Control kills dreams, and it is responsible for stealing peace and joy from the lives of people. Control has ripped apart marriages and caused families to crumble. Controlling leaders have stifled the call of God in people's lives, causing them to live in constant fear of their leadership. The spirit of control is unhappy unless everyone around has submitted their lives, will, and future under its grip. This has been running rampant in the Pentecostal church world for far too long. Men and women of God must begin to call it out for what it is—unhealthy and ungodly. Control in a person can be defeated only once it is confronted and exposed.

"The biggest opponent to the spirit of revival is the spirit of control." – Rodney Howard-Browne[5]

When control is confronted, it usually means the war is on its way. When Elijah stood up to Jezebel, she was angered and shocked that he would not bow to her tactics of control and manipulation. But Elijah knew the power of God was greater than Jezebel and her controlling, wicked spirit.

Control is not limited to the pulpit. You probably don't have to look much farther than your family or circle of friends to find at least one individual who operates in the spirit of control—causing other family members great fear of their reactions to decisions. I've been approached by grown men terrified to tell their mother that they want to marry the woman of their dreams because *momma didn't approve of her.* I've talked to women who are stricken with fear when they consider the reaction that their father will have when he found out that she doesn't want to carry on the family business.

To Control or Not To Control

In Christ, and with the right motives, there can be such a healthy balance within the church when dealing with leading the flock. Yes,

I believe that submission and authority are godly principles for every Christian believer. But, healthy submission and authority is widely different than unhealthy submission and authority. The difference between healthy and unhealthy submission and authority are the motivation behind the one leading and the one being led.

First and foremost, every Christian believer should place themselves under the submission and authority of our Head, Jesus. That means that every individual believer has been given their own free will, the mind of Christ, and the ability to make decisions, based on the depth of their relationship with Him. I cannot think of one example in the New Testament that Jesus acted toward or taught and instructed his disciples out of fear of losing them to the next Rabbi.

Jesus never held them back from going out to fulfill their destiny. In fact, Jesus not only sent them out into their destinies, but He then gave them the power and authority in which to go out—and it didn't take fifteen years of the disciples sitting under His ministry and leadership before "they were ready" to be released.

"And He called the twelve to Himself, and began to send them out two by two, and gave them power over unclean spirits" (Mark 6:7 NKJV).

"After these things the Lord appointed seventy others also, and sent them two by two before His face into every city and place where He Himself was about to go" (Luke 10:1).

I have lived through the shepherding movement and I have witnessed, first hand, the wide spread damage that has been caused by insecure leaders who are bent on controlling their flock—all under the false understanding of submission.

I understand, the shepherding movement was an extremely skewed example of the godly submission in our leaders. But, even outside of the shepherding movement, this unhealthy distortion of the truth exists. Some of our closest friends have chosen the shackles of fear and control over the dream and destiny that once burned in their hearts, all because of the strong arm and wrong motives of their leadership. They yoke themselves to their leaders and excuse their inaction of fulfilling God's plan for their life, by their belief that,

"Well, God brought me to this church and placed me under this leadership. And God will tell my pastor when I am ready to be sent out."

I can understand this type of control as well as anyone. For a time, I was part of a church that was well versed at hanging the noose of control on its congregants. The pressure was applied from the pulpit on down to the pews and countless underlying sermons were preached daring anyone to *leave the group*. For fear of losing their place in the will of God, many chose instead to forfeit their own ministries and future ministry.

The pressure to never leave the group was applied so thick, and I watched as those who dared to leave were cut off completely. Long time friendships from those who left the group, for any reason, were dissolved. The relationship between the church, its leaders, and the family who left, was symbolically burned in one last final act of control. When we too, eventually felt the Holy Spirit moving us out of that church and city, the same thing happened to us and then to so many others who have left since then.

We were ministering in a conference near the United States and Canadian border. One night, after an amazing night of God's power and presence, a lady in the church began to share with us about her calling to be an evangelist. She told us that as a young girl, her grandmother took her to a Kathryn Kuhlman meeting. In that meeting, Kathryn laid her hands on her and prophesied that one day she too, would travel the whole country, preaching about the fire of God. Now in her late 50s, this lady was perplexed as to why God hadn't yet allowed her ministry to come to fruition.

We asked her a few more questions and we soon learned that she had been a member in her current church for over thirty years. She explained that years ago, she shared with her pastor that she was called to be an evangelist. He told her then that she should wait, sit under his ministry for a while, and learn how ministry was done.

Occasionally, her pastor would allow her to speak to the young ladies in the church youth group, or to the woman's fellowship group. She said that she grew content for some years when her pastor finally asked her to lead the children's ministry of the church for a few years. Every so often she would ask her pastor to "release" her and allow her to begin her evangelistic ministry. And each time she did, her pastor had another excuse why *now* wasn't the right time. Eventually, the fire waned and the dream fell dormant in her heart.

Now, years later, she was filled with regret. It wasn't God that didn't allow her to fulfill her calling in the ministry. She was to blame, and so was her pastor. For all these years, she had relied on the leader of her church to inform her of *when she was ready*, rather than relying on the Leader of the church, Jesus. Unknowingly, she had allowed her pastor to put to death the calling given to her by Jesus as part of her inheritance and legacy.

Healthy submission is a beautiful and wonderful gift that is designed to help train, equip, and guide us on the right path. My wife and I have certain people and ministries that we have asked to speak into our lives, give us exhortation, rebuke us, if necessary, and set us right again. These men and women have motives that are right. We are able to recognize their motives, because in every circumstance they have been encouraging, and their insight has pushed us to go forward, further stepping out onto the waters of faith. That is a picture of healthy, godly submission. Their aim is not to keep us back, but rather to help us extend our reach farther for the Kingdom of Heaven.

> *"... His divine power has given to us all things that pertain to life and godliness, through the knowledge of Him who called us by glory and virtue, by which have been given to us exceedingly great and precious promises, that through these you may be partakers of the divine nature..."* (II Peter 1:3-4a NKJV).

If anyone, whether it be your pastor, parent, friend, colleague, teacher, coach or counselor, speaks into you a word or advice that is contrary to the word of the Lord spoken to you by God—follow God. The motives of our Heavenly Father are flawlessly pure. His desire for you is to live your life with purpose and with power. He has called you to fulfill His great commission. He has already given you all the things that pertain to life and to godliness. He has made you to be the light of the world. You are the city that He has placed on a hill that cannot be hidden. You are the chosen and you are an heir *with* Christ. Nothing is impossible for you. You CAN do it!

When I was a young teenager, my youth pastor heard that I had in my heart the desire for full-time ministry. Even though I only had two years of Bible College under my belt, God used him to constantly push me to step outside of fear and run toward the high calling in Christ Jesus. I can remember one of the last things he said to me before I entered the ministry, "It's better to have tried and failed, then to not try at all, because not trying is failing anyway."

I know that some people may disagree with my stand on the issue of submission and authority within the church. In the evangelistic ministry I meet many different pastors and church leaders, from many different denominations, rivers, and groups. They don't always agree with me, and I don't always agree with them. Paul and Barnabas were a great example of two ministries disagreeing. They had differences in their ministry approach and their ministry philosophy, but they didn't concern themselves by degrading each other or cursing one another with gossip and a controlling spirit.

Our pastor is a constant encouragement to us, and he humbly gives his input and wisdom, even in times that he may disagree, of which we are forever grateful. Our pastor is Dr. Rodney-Howard Browne. He has endured over twenty years of church leaders who bash him, trying to control him and discourage him in the ministry. Yet, he is constant. He also has had trustworthy, well-known ministers, speak into his life, yielding a greater and healthy hunger for more of God and to see Christ's church run hard after the anointing of the Holy Spirit in their lives.

Control from the Pews

Sure, I have seen many controlling church leaders, but truthfully, I have seen far more controlling pew warmers—people in the church bent on controlling the pastor and church leaders. Like in the story I told you about my friend, Pastor Bruce, I've also seen church leaders and board members fighting to control the pastor and his or her every decision.

Control is wicked, but self-control is divine. Do you realize that the only control that we are instructed to exert toward anyone, is control over our own spirit and body? Revival is about man, losing control over everything except for the discipline over his own flesh and his own spirit. There is no room in revival for control over the Holy Spirit, or over our leadership, our flock, our spouse, or even over our children.

"But if you are led by the Spirit, you are not under the law" (Galatians 5:18 NKJV).

Leading is not the same as controlling. The Holy Spirit led Jesus into the wilderness; Paul the Apostle was led on his missions by the Holy Spirit. The Holy Spirit does not control you. You do not control the Holy Spirit. Godly submission says, "I yield my life to the will of the Holy Spirit, because I trust that He will lead me to where I must go."

Pull Off the Covers

The only way to defeat control in your life is by confronting and exposing it for what it is—wicked and ungodly. Maybe you have a controlling church leadership, or perhaps you are guilty of trying to manipulate and control the decisions of your pastors and church leaders. Are you busy trying to micro-control your family, your marriage, your home, to the point that you are driving everyone away?

A controlling person is fueled on when it is left unchecked, not confronted, and not overcome. It can seem easier to stay controlled or to continue controlling others, than it is to be confrontational and expose the spirit of control to the light of the Holy Spirit.

Control freaks come in all kinds and in all sorts of people. They come in the form of our bosses and colleagues, spouses and parents, spiritual leaders and elders, and even those in governmental positions and places of business. That controlling, Jezebel spirit will only be satisfied when it is given its own way, have its own opinion rule, and to lord over as many people as possible.

"Thus says the Lord of hosts: I am jealous for Zion with great jealousy, and I am jealous for her with great wrath [against her enemies]." (Zechariah 8:2, AMP).

Godly submission and authority is a beautiful thing. Outside of the grip of control, our passions toward God can soar and revival can thrive and produce. Passion can only grow outside the limitations of control, because that is where revival exists.

In this hour, we must guard the passionate fire within our heart. It is critical that we no longer submit our lives to religious people who lack the pure passion for revival. Leave behind religious traditions, no matter how powerful they may have once been. Stop returning to the bondage, from which we've been made free through the powerful grace of Jesus Christ.

Coloring Outside the Lines

God's presence does not operate within the lines of a structured, man-made system of religious rules, guidelines, and opinions. As fun as it may seem for a child to color within the coloring book lines, it is the opposite in the realm of God's supernatural presence and power.

God is not at all concerned with staying *inside the lines* of religion or people's opinions. I have found that often it is the exact opposite, and the presence of God (revival) is positioned intentionally outside the lines of man. This is especially true when it comes to believers who are aflame with excited, passionate zeal for God. These people never stay inside the lines of the religious norm.

"God spoke to me years ago, 'Look at what the church is doing nationwide and do the opposite...'" – Dr. Rodney Howard-Browne[6]

Common Denominator

The common denominator of all new Christian believers is their passion for God. They have been forgiven of so much that their hearts swell with passion, aroused by the grace and heart of God. To them, the sky seems bluer, the grass looks greener, and life is more worth living, just because of what Jesus did for them.

Zeal and passion for God shines like the bright lights of a city that have been set on a hill. Everyone can see the city for its bright shining light. Then comes religion. The objective of religion is to locate and eradicate any sign of the joy of the Lord in our lives. Slowly and subtly it approaches, with its death hold it tries to fasten to us like the grip of a python. Its goal is to drain all the passion and excitement, leaving us lifeless and bored.

I will never forget the time that we were invited to minister in a denominational church in New England. As we drove into the church parking lot, we were instantly met and greeted by a middle-aged couple from the church. They helped us get some of our belongings out from the car and we talked with them briefly. Standing with them outside the church building for a few minutes, we talked and laughed. They seemed like happy people, even expressing to us their enthusiastic appreciation for us to come and minister at their church.

Then, together with them, we entered the church. Once we entered into the building I noticed something about the couple had changed. As I looked at them, it seemed that the very life in them that we saw outside the building had been robbed from them. They transformed into somber, sad, and depressed people right before our eyes, and within seconds. It was like an episode of *The Twilight Zone*.

As we all made our way into the sanctuary, we noticed an odor in the air. It smelled moldy, musty, and old. Clearly, the sanctuary hadn't seen a paint job in over forty years. The only thing to match the odor in the building was the stench of religion that permeated the room. Susie and I looked at each other and smiled. We knew we were going to have to get out the *big revival guns* to bust this place free of their religion.

Worship started and it was sad. I thought that maybe God was dead, and no one bothered to tell us about it. Perhaps at any moment we might see His coffin roll down the center aisle. I looked around and noticed that some of the men had started early with their Sunday church nap.

After worship was over, I asked Susie to greet the people. On the countenance of most people was written depression, and there was no joy to be found in the room. With her whole heart, Susie passionately charged them to get ready, because God was about to rip out the death and infuse life into their hearts. She said, "This week, you will experience a fresh touch of God. He is going to reach into this place and pull the poison of religion out of your life. He is going to restore to you the joy of your salvation that has been stolen by religious tradition and control." No one made a move.

With that, Susie handed me the microphone. I almost wanted to say to the people, "Wasn't that a nice service? You're dismissed." Instead of giving in to the desire of my flesh, I obeyed the Holy Spirit. "Tom," the Holy Spirit spoke to my heart, "Raise the dead!" With those instructions, I preached my heart out, and "raise the dead" is what we did that week.

Throughout the week, one by one, the people softened their hearts again toward God. Those who didn't want to change stayed away from the rest of the week's meetings. But, those who wanted to break free from the clutch of dead, lifeless religion attended every service. Many arrived early and stayed late into the night, soaking in the presence of God.

On the final night of the week, we received a phone call in our hotel room a few hours before the service was to begin. The couple that we had met in the parking lot the first night called to share from their heart. They told us how this week had revolutionized their spiritual life and their marriage too. They had repented to God because, after years, they finally realized that they had been living with passion for everything else, and none for Jesus.

That week we challenged that spirit of religion toe-to-toe in that church. Many had become captive to sin and apathy because somewhere after their salvation they had lost their passion for Jesus.

Guarding the Passion

I love to use the analogy of a campfire when relating to revival. The different elements that make up the campfire can represent the different elements to revival. For example, when lit, a campfire is not going to infinitely burn. Something must be done to start the fire and something must be done to keep the fire burning.

Fire is a word we use to describe passion—fire *for* God and passion *for* God—fire *of* God and passion *of* God. The fire of God burning within us must be guarded and allowed to keep on burning or it will eventually be put out.

Revival in our life is a precious, precious thing. Guarding it is essential and necessary. We can guard it many different ways. We can pray and fast; read and fellowship with the Holy Spirit. We can shut off the voices of doubt and complacency from the halfhearted and religious. We can turn away from the control of men and women who will choke out any signs of life. We can surround ourselves with others who are hungry like us and even hungrier than us. We can travel to places where revival fire is burning hot, and we can partake of their fire to keep our passion ablaze.

"The fear of man brings a snare, but whoever trusts in the Lord shall be safe" (Proverbs 29:25 NKJV).

All of these things will help to guard the passionate fire of God in our heart. But, above all else, once we have hold of the passion of God, we must protect it at all cost.

"... but one thing I do, forgetting those things which are behind and reaching forward to those things which are ahead, I press toward the goal for the prize of the upward call of God in Christ Jesus. Therefore let us, as many as are mature, have this mind;..." (Philippians 3:13-15 NKJV)

CHAPTER 10
THOSE FUNNY MANIFESTATIONS

Let me begin this chapter with my experience of the supernatural manifestation of laughter that fell on me for the first time in 1996. This supernatural manifestation was transforming to my life. I was in a season of transition in ministry. I had already pioneered a growing church in New Jersey, before moving to California to pastor, and with a decade of full-time ministry behind me, I was only thirty years old.

I had just finished an extended fast and I grew desperately hungry and thirsty for more demonstrations of God's power in my life than ever before. For years, I had grown weary of fighting in the church and the usual church politics. I hoped to never hear another person complain about the volume of the worship, color of the carpet, or length of the meetings. I had just dealt with some of the adults in my church who were complaining about the youth group, because the youth were gathering to pray at the front altar before the service. While the youth were about their Father's business, the adults wanted to be able to fellowship with one another, and evidently, the adults couldn't hear themselves above the zealous prayers of the youth group.

I had my fill and I was at the end of my rope with the foolish games played in the church. The pressure and stress of church silliness had warn heavily on my heart. About that time, a friend of mine invited me to go with him to a nearby church where an evangelist by the name of Richard Moore, was holding revival outpouring meetings. I hardly could believe my friend when he explained that this evangelist had been ministering for six weeks straight, and the meetings were growing every day. By now, the hunger in my heart was exploding. I was desperate for God to do something different in me, and knowing God, I tried to ready myself for anything.

We arrived to the church on time, but when we walked into the building we realized that the sanctuary was nearly full. An usher told us that unless we wanted to stand for the duration meeting, we could not sit with each other. That was fine, so the usher took each of us to our respective seats. The meeting began, the worship was good, but nothing extravagant. Then the evangelist took the microphone to collect the offering. As he shared on the importance of giving, I began to laugh. Nothing was funny. He wasn't cracking jokes. "Why am I laughing?" I thought to myself.

The more the evangelist spoke, the more I laughed. I couldn't seem to get a hold of myself. Within a few minutes, I was laughing uncontrollably. The more I tried to stop it, the louder I would bellow. I thought to myself, "What is this?" I felt like I was drunk. Nothing made any sense to me, but everything was funny. I grew more embarrassed by the moment.

Before long, the young teen-aged boy seated next to me, started to laugh. Slow at first, but quickly he too was belting out in screams of laughter. Just when my laughing would gently subside, he would roar up again and I couldn't help but follow.

Finally, the evangelist called for the ushers to pick me up and stand me in the center isle of the church. I was so *drunk in the Spirit* that I couldn't even stand up without the help of the ushers. Four big men with usher vests quickly scooped me up and stood me in the center aisle. Then the evangelist raised his hand, pointed his finger at me like a gun, and shouted, "FIRE!"

Instantly, the power of God blew me back, knocking all four of the ushers down with me to the ground. For the rest of the night, I remain there, laying on the floor under a heavy blanket of the presence of God. It felt like light volts of electricity coursing through my body. They were warm, welcoming currents of God's love. I would begin to weep as I lay there on the floor, and then I would laugh again. Over and over, I could feel the Holy Spirit as He was restoring to me the joy of my salvation that had been robbed by years in the church.

The next morning when I awoke, I couldn't remember getting home the night before. All I could do was marvel at how this strange manifestation of the Holy Spirit had so deeply touched me. I had never experienced laughter like that before, and certainly never in church. But, by it, I had been transformed, and I could feel myself falling more and more in love with Jesus Christ.

Why Manifestations?

"There are diversities of gifts, but the same Spirit. There are differences of ministries, but the same Lord. And there are diversities of activities, but it is the same God who works all in all. But the manifestation of the Spirit is given to each one for the profit of all" (1 Corinthians 12:4-7 NKJV).

So many people want the power and presence of God to touch their lives, as long as they can stay in control of their surrounding and their emotions. With God, this is impossible. Manifestations are given so that we are able to lose our grip of this world and connect to the heavily realm.

I Corinthians chapter 12 tells us, "the manifestation of the Spirit is given …" The Holy Spirit gives us these manifestations. They are often times, signs and wonders, given to the church, in order to provoke the church toward new revelations and experiences in God.

I Corinthians chapter 12 also tells us, "the manifestation of the Spirit is given to each one *for the profit of all.*" God's heart is not limited to just your experience with His manifestations. So often, people become self-centered and ask God for the manifestations in order to be blessed themselves. And God does want to bless you, but He also wants to bless those around you. He will give you these manifestations as a blessing to you, and He will give you these manifestations to bless and touch others, that they might also believe.

Several years ago, during a brief time of discouragement, I attended a conference in British Columbia, Canada. I had not told anyone, except my wife, that I had been battling with discouragement and that my outlook was downcast. She encouraged me to go, get away with God, and see what He might have to say about the future.

I was sitting in the back of the auditorium while others were shouting, dancing, and singing to the Lord. That night I was being selfish and my attitude was bad. I didn't want to engage in worship with the rest of the crowd, so I sat down and watched. As the worship continued, I noticed a large group of Japanese believers, who had traveled from Tokyo to attend the conference. They were lining the steps of the church balcony. As I was watching them, my eye caught the site of one Japanese woman near the top of the group. She was laughing, obviously drunk in the Spirit.

As she stood there laughing, she began to swing her arm in a circle, like a windmill. At first, I thought to myself how foolish she looked, but the longer I watched her, I began to laugh and then cry. I sat there in my chair in the back of the sanctuary laughing and crying, and laughing and crying, until I felt all the grief and discouragement leave my heart. After about thirty minutes, I cleared the tears from my eyes and looked up in her direction again. By now, she had stopped, and she was standing, raising her hands and weeping before the Lord.

Because this Japanese woman yielded to the presence of God, the manifestation of the Holy Spirit was given to her, for my profit. She had no idea that the manifestation of the Spirit that she had that night, actually had nothing to do with her; although I am sure she was also blessed. Instead, the manifestation of the Spirit was given to her for my profit.

Understanding
the Manifestations of the Spirit

There are many different ways that the Holy Spirit manifests Himself in us, on us, to us, and through us. We can study the Scriptures and read church history to learn of all the wonderful effects of the manifestations of the Spirit.

Sometimes, the manifestation of the Spirit is given to an individual to be a prophetic sign to them and to those around them. Another way of understanding the manifestation of the Spirit is to recognize that our natural body cannot contain all of God's power flowing through it, and because of that, our body has a reaction. Manifestations can be described as, a supernatural God invading natural man's body.

Electricity is a great example. Imagine, natural electricity invading your body. The intense current of that energy would cause your natural body to react. As a result, you may shake, fall to the ground, and so on. The same is true, that when the God who created electricity, touches you with His power, then your body cannot help but react to that power.

Some of the most common Biblical and historical (church history) occurrences of manifestations of the Spirit include, shaking, weeping, laughing, tongues, trances and visions, falling to the ground, rolling, jerking, and translations in the spirit.

Perhaps you have never personally experienced any of these manifestations, but your lack of experience with them does not negate the reality and truth of them. These are manifestations that we should hunger to experience, and welcome when they come. There is nothing to fear from these strange manifestations, after all, they've been given to us by our loving heavenly Father, who gives us every good and perfect gift from above.

Since the Charismatic Renewal of the mid-1960s, the Charismatic church is very well aware of people falling *under the power* or going into *spiritual "dormition."* Fifty years of witnessing this phenomenon, to us, is no longer alarming. In our meetings, it is almost *normal* in every service to see such a manifestation of the Spirit, especially during times of prayer ministry. Walk into almost any of our meetings and you will see people weeping, laughing, rocking, or laying on the floor under the influence of the Holy Spirit. The same common manifestations can be seen in many mainstream Pentecostal churches.

In the 1990s, we know of people like Dr. Rodney Howard-Browne, and others such as the *Toronto Blessing* that were known for strange manifestations of laughter and joy in the church services. These specific manifestations of the Spirit have been seen periodically throughout church history. For example, John Wesley's wife was known to have laughed uncontrollably in the Spirit many times. In the Great Awakening of the 1700s in America, and during the Azusa Street revival in 1906, it is recorded that holy laughter was a usual happening among believers and seekers of the Holy Spirit, just like today. As we yield to the Holy Spirit in manifestations, we will see them increase more and more.

"You Can't Handle the Truth"

In the mid-1990s, after my experience with this manifestation of the joy of the Lord, we have seen an increase of people, all over the world, getting touched with the manifestation of the Spirit, in laughter.

In Minneapolis, Minnesota, we were ministering in an, all black, inner-city church. On the first night, the music minister (who was eight months pregnant) became so drunk in the Spirit that she laughed on the floor of the church for hours. She laughed and rolled around on the floor so much, that her hair extensions started falling out, and her make-up had smeared and ran amuck all over her face. Even her dress was disheveled and wrinkling. She laughed so hard and for so long that night, that she had to be lifted and carried out of the church by her husband and three other men.

As they picked her up to carry her out, her arms were still moving and she looked like she was swimming out the door. God's power had so touched her, that her physical body was reacting. What no one there knew that night, except for her and her husband, is that she had seen the doctor earlier that morning about her pregnancy. Her doctor told them that the umbilical cord had wrapped itself around the neck of the baby, and the doctors best diagnosis was that if the child didn't die, it would at least be born with severe brain damage.

Hearing this news, this woman of great faith wanted to give God a chance. That night she came to our service expecting God's power to work in her belly.

Her husband drove her home while she laughed, cried, and shook under the power of God. When he put her into bed, she was still drunk in the Spirit and shaking like a wild woman. That night, he didn't sleep a wink because of her shaking and laughing while she slept. The next day, he returned home from work in time to take her to church again. To his amazement, she was still drunk in the Spirit and needed to be carried to church.

Night after night, she received prayer ministry, and night after night, God's power reached deeper. None of us knew in what manner or for what profit God was touching her life so powerfully.

Ten days after the last revival meeting at her church, she gave birth to a totally healthy baby boy. Her doctors were amazed. There was no sign of brain damage. Through the manifestation of the Spirit on this woman, God was healing the child living in her womb.

"This beginning of signs Jesus did in Cana of Galilee, and manifested His glory; and His disciples believed in Him" (John 2:11 NKJV).

CHAPTER 11
DON'T TOUCH
MY TREASURE!

What is wrong with talking about money and offerings in the church? Well, in most Evangelical, Charismatic, and even Pentecostal churches, the offering is usually considered "taboo." Offerings are frequently relegated to a box in the back of the church, or a quick pass of the bucket in an effort to quickly get that uncomfortable part of the service out of the way. There is no doubt that money, or the subject of finances, is often looked upon as unspiritual and unimportant. But, do you realize that Jesus spoke on the subjects of finances, money, investing, and offerings, more often than He spoke about clean moral living, raising the dead, walking on water, fasting, and even miracles?

That being said, I have long realized that our spiritual maturity is not just dependent upon our worship, hunger, or how many times we attend church services—it is equally dependent upon our giving. Giving is a key attribute in the life of Kingdom believers, and without the revelation and the practice of liberal giving we stunt our own spiritual growth.

Our mentality, the way we view a thing, will either limit us or release us to greater, grander things. Poverty is a mentality, and it will surely limit your direction and destiny, but prosperity is also a mentality, and it will help propel you and your destiny in God to greater heights than you could ever have imagined.

I learned this truth some years ago, October 2002 to be exact. I had already been seasoned in the ministry for many years and, financially speaking, I was never able to imagine myself outside of "barely getting by." Over the years I had grown content with what I thought the life of a minister must be, poor. At this time, Susie and I were engaged to be married and together there were a great number of things we wished and dreamed to accomplish for the Kingdom of God—so many places we wanted to bring the Gospel, but deep down I was discouraged because I knew that "barely getting by" didn't pay well enough to fund those wishes and dreams.

A close friend of mine called me one afternoon to invite me to join him at a ministerial conference with Dr. Rodney Howard-Browne at The River in Tampa, Florida the following week. As he gave me the details of the conference, I could feel a strong desire in my heart and although I didn't know why, I knew that somehow I must get there. The next week, I scrapped up the funds and bought my ticket. I boarded the plane and was on my way.

I'll never forget what happened as my friend and I walked into the building that first night. It was as if the room was alive with anticipation and expectation in the people's hearts. We were shown to our seats, right in the front row. The worship started and I quickly got lost in the Spirit.

"If people don't catch the spirit of giving, then they will never catch the spirit of revival." – Dr. Rodney Howard-Browne[7]

After the worship team sat down, Dr. Rodney Howard-Browne began to speak on the offering. It was thirty minutes later and he was still teaching on the offering. He called it, *Breaking Free from a Poverty Mentality*. I thought to myself, "He sure is taking a long time on the offering teaching." I was hoping he would wrap this offering thing up and get to the main message. Just as that thought crossed my mind, he stopped and stood directly in front of my seat and said, "Some of you here tonight are wishing that I would get off of this offering message and get onto the main message. I have news for you, THIS IS the main message!"

There was no doubt in my mind that God was speaking and I knew I needed to listen. I said in my heart, "Lord, I need You to speak to me. I need You to show me how to go to another level." My mind was whirling around as the message continued for over another hour. People were weeping all over the building. Some were laughing, and some were clearly angry that he would take so much time teaching about money in church, but I knew God wanted me here so that He could change me. I just didn't realize that it was my mentality that He wanted changed.

The first night after the service, my friend and I joined Pastor Rodney and some of the other ministers for a bite to eat. Everyone laughed and talked, enjoying each other's company and fellowship. As I was preparing to leave and retire to my hotel room, Pastor Rodney looked at me and said, "Tom, you have a great anointing, but the wrong mentality. This week, God is going to impart something in you and with it, you will start to take men and women of God to the outer limits of their minds."

The next day, my heart was still stirring from the message the previous night. My heart was swelling with faith and excitement for what God was about to impart to me.

The final night, I went to the church early to pray. I told God that I needed clear direction for the ministry and that I was willing to do whatever He asked. I told Him that I trusted Him to use Pastor Rodney's sermons that night to answer my heart's questions. Soon the service began with erupting worship and the presence of God came to us so strong and powerful.

Pastor Rodney took us to Luke chapter 4, and again he spoke once again about *"Breaking the Spirit of Poverty."* He said, "The way to break a spirit of anything is to move in the opposite spirit. The way to break that mentality of poverty in your ministry is not by praying over it. It is broken by GIVING!"

I sat on the edge of my seat eating every word from the man of God. He spoke that night as a prophet and not as a pastor, and his words were dipped in fresh fire for us all. As he preached I spoke to God in my heart, "Lord, I don't have much money. I already gave everything I had in the offering, so how can You ask me to give more?"

It was almost midnight and Pastor Rodney was still preaching. The power of God was manifesting in different ways to several people. About that time, Pastor Rodney turned to me and said, "Come here my friend…"

"Within twelve months from this day, as you look back upon your ministry you'll say, 'I cannot believe the transformation that's taken place, I cannot believe the change,' because it will seem like you're light years ahead of where you are. The Lord says He will make up for the years that you've lost. I hear the Lord say He's going to make up for the years the enemy has stolen, and I'm going to launch you within these twelve months—five years ahead. Fire! You're going to run like you've never run before with the glory of God. Father, I thank you for it right now—New Doors—New Day—New Realm!" – Prophecy given me by Rodney Howard-Browne (October 10, 2002)

For hours into the early morning, I lay on the floor of that church under the power of God. I wept and laughed as I felt the Holy Spirit burning these changes into my soul. As I finally got myself up from the carpeted floor, I purposed to live a life and ministry free from a poverty mentality. I determined to walk boldly with a mentality of prosperity and liberal, generous giving. Never again would I be subject to lack. My God was big and mighty and now so was I.

Within the year, Susie and I were married and together we watched as our ministry exploded with a tremendous five-hundred percent growth, exactly as it was prophesied that night in October 2002.

The Poverty Mentality

In Matthew chapter 6, our Lord Jesus taught us that our treasure was located in the same place as our heart. Regardless of what you may have been taught in Sunday School, your heart is not where your tambourine is. Your heart is not where your banner or shofar is. Your heart is in the exact location as your treasure.

Do you want to find out where your heart is? That is easy — just take a look at your checkbook or your bank statement. Where is your money going? Find out where your money is going and that is where you'll find your heart. Is your money consistently being spent putting a little white ball into a hole on the course? Is it constantly used up at the mall? I promise you, that wherever you are putting your money, THAT IS where your heart is. Remember, this is coming from a normal guy who enjoys golf and even the occasional trip to the mall. But, answer honestly, can your treasure and your heart be found in Kingdom business or in the temporal pleasures of this world?

Sadly enough, many ministries know that people's hearts are so attached to their money that they resort to using *gimmicks*. Christian television is notorious for schemes like sending water from the Jordan River in exchange for an offering donation. I have even known of some ministries charging God's saints for a prophetic word.

Jesus constantly taught on finances, money, and giving, because He knew it was a sure way to locate people spiritually.

"Do not lay up for yourselves treasures on earth, where moth and rust destroy and where thieves break in and steal; but lay up for yourselves treasures in heaven, where neither moth nor rust destroys and where thieves do not break in and steal. For where your treasure is, there your heart will be also. The lamp of the body is the eye. If therefore your eye is good, your whole body will be full of light. But if your eye is bad, your whole body will be full of darkness. If therefore the light that is in you is darkness, how great is that darkness! No one can serve two masters; for either he will hate the one and love the other, or else he will be loyal to the one and despise the other. You cannot serve God and mammon" (Matthew 6:19-24 NKJV).

Jesus taught about our treasure, and then He immediately started talking about *"The lamp of the body is the eye. If therefore your eye is good, your whole body will be full of light. But if your eye is bad, your whole body will be full of darkness. If therefore the light that is in you is darkness, how great is that darkness!"*

It sounds like Jesus was speaking in riddles, but He wasn't. At the time of His teaching here, Jesus was not speaking to folks from the 21st century. He was speaking to Jews who lived in a very Jewish culture. This was a Jewish idiom that referred to a person's generosity or lack of generosity. Jesus spoke to them in a way that they could best understand Him. It means that the lamp of the body was the eye. If your eye was good — if you are generous, then the path of your spiritual life would be full of light and well lit. But if your eye was bad, meaning ungenerous and stingy, then your spiritual life would be full of darkness.

"For to everyone who has, more will be given, and he will have abundance; but from him who does not have, even what he has will be taken away" (Matthew 25:29 NKJV).

Jesus taught that MORE would be given to the one who already has. That does not sound *fair* to the socialistic or communistic mentality, but it is a Biblical pattern. Socialistic politicians try their best to convince the public that equal distribution of wealth is the cure to poverty. The only message they try harder to publish is that those in power within the government should be the ones to equally distribute the wealth. Thankfully, God has a better mentality—the best, in fact. God says that the one who has will be given more. Why? Because he is faithful with what he already has—he is faithful to grow it into more and he is faithful to sow it into God's Kingdom. The one who has is given even more because he has been wise to gain more, and so he will be blessed with more. What some people may consider *unfair* is considered right to God, and He is the best qualified to decide who gets what and why.

Guess what? Winning the lottery or gaining a great inheritance of money will never set you free from a poverty mentality. Being crowned king or president doesn't necessarily make you a prosperous thinker. The only way to truly transition from poverty to prosperity is in your mind, in your thinking. You must despise the poverty mentality that sets you back from moving forward and gaining greater ground in life. I tell you this from experience. Before the day that our whole ministry was transformed, I was stuck in the rut of a poverty mindset. I realized then that in order to change my outcome, I had to change my mindset. I realized that I would never have until I began to form a lifestyle of generosity, giving, and planting seed.

I started to hate the fact that I had lived with junk mentality and that I didn't live with the spirit of excellence that I so badly needed. There was a total transformation in me when I caught the spirit of giving and I began to change the way I thought. I was no longer giving into the offering bucket, now I was sowing into the Kingdom, knowing that as I did so, God was able to give me even more. I am now a faithful steward.

God loves prosperity and He lives in prosperity. Prosperity and financial blessing are not in opposition to revival, rather they are directly involved and tied together with revival. Giving does not begin and end with our finances, but giving goes right through onto evangelism, prayer, fasting, worship, and so on. We must be liberal givers in every part of life.

Some believers have such a poverty mindset that they cannot handle when God dares to touch their treasure. When the minister speaks about opening their pocketbook in church, the offense becomes tangible. This is true all over the world. I've seen it over and over again. Don't be like those believers. Be different. Be free. Be like God. Be liberal in your giving.

I truly challenge you to allow the Holy Spirit to supernaturally change you. Allow His truth to touch your treasure and change your treasure. As you release your treasure into His trustworthy hands, then your heart is being released to God in so many new ways. I had to allow the Holy Spirit to offend my mind in this area of giving, blessing, and prosperity, before I was able to see our ministry explode. My heart was opened to allow God to do more in me so that He could do more through me.

Debt Cancellation

We were invited to minister at a church for one week. That week turned into two and then into three. On the final night, during the fourth week, I told the people to bring their bills to the front of the church. With great faith and anticipation I prophesied to the people. I told them that as I prayed over their bills that night, they would see great miracles in the weeks to follow. There was an assembly of people there that night who were excited and expectant for God to do wonders in their finances. I asked the people to stretch their hands over their finances and pray with me. A shout of prayer and praise erupted as we prayed over every financial obligation and need represented.

My office administrator called me on the road, the following week, to share with me that testimonies of financial miracles and blessings were flooded into the ministry office. One elderly lady testified that her bank called her to tell her that someone, not a family member, walked into the bank and paid off her home. In that same week, a young man had someone walk into his bank and paid off his entire bank note of over $22,000 for his pickup truck.

Week after week, for three months, testimonies like these continued to stream into our office. We have literally seen millions of dollars blessed into the hands of God's people. One man had an invention that we prayed over that night. Two months later, the man called to tell us that he was granted a contract from a home shopping television channel that was willing to pay him 3.5 million dollars to sell his product.

God used the Old Testament prophets, Elijah and Elisha to pray, and people debts were cancelled. God is the same today and He can use New Testament man or woman to pray with the same results. Settle in your mind and in your heart now, today, that if God were to bless you with a large amount of finances in the next few weeks, then how much of it does He get? When you are able to settle that question, and knowing that you will be faithful not to spend it on your own lusts, then you know that God can trust you.

Entrepreneur Spirit

"And thou hast remembered Jehovah thy God, for He it is who is giving to thee power to make wealth, in order to establish His covenant which He hath sworn to thy fathers as at this day" (Deuteronomy 8:17-18 YLT).

We were ministering in New Jersey and I felt again in my spirit to pray over people's finances. I encouraged the people by sharing that God desired to bless them by starting your own businesses. While I was preaching, a young teenager told his mother, "I am going to do that. I am going to start my own business." He already had a job working at McDonald's, but his mother encouraged him to trust God for a business of his own. One month later, the young, sixteen year old boy started a computer business out of his parents garage.

Six months later, we received a call from this mother. While she spoke to me on the phone, she reminded me that I had encouraged them that God wanted to give them businesses. She shared that her son was there that night and had decided to start his own computer company out of their family garage. Now, six months later, he had made over $100,000 and was on track to earn almost $250,000 by the years end. She was stunned by this goodness of God, and she admitted that her sixteen year old son was now making more money than she and her husband were making combined.

God wants to pour blessing upon us, but often He wants to build within us a faith, a confidence, and an entrepreneurial spirit that will show us to not just *get a job,* but to *create a job.* The Bible tells us that God has given us the power to create wealth.

Sow into Your Destiny

We must financially give with purpose. This is an important part of the Kingdom of God. Jesus was the greatest offering that God ever gave to humanity. Let us learn to give just like our Heavenly Father gives. He didn't give the world His only Son in secret or hidden in shame. He was offered up in front of the whole world, and He was sown as a seed. Jesus, the only Son of God, was sown as a seed. The Bible says that He was sown so that God could reap many sons in return.

God believes in prosperity and so He sowed His best seed. He sowed his ONLY son, so that He could reap MANY sons. Giving is meant to unleash multiplication for the Kingdom of God, and God loves to get the glory when people are blessed.

Giving is one of the most spiritual things you can do. Never think that offering time is an unspiritual act that must be done just to keep the lights on in the church. That wicked, poverty mentality must be challenged and changed by the power of the cross. The message of the cross is so very great—the sacrifice of One meant the freedom of all. Your giving, your generous and sacrificial giving, will mean freedom for others. That is a principle of God's Kingdom. To God, giving is always central and it was His gift that led you to God Himself.

CHAPTER 12
BIBLICAL
CHURCH GROWTH

"So continuing daily with one accord in the temple, breaking bread from house to house, they ate their food with gladness and simplicity of heart, praising God and having favor with all the people. And the Lord added to the church daily those who were being saved" (Acts 2:46-47 NKJV).

Growth is at the very core of revival. I have heard so many definitions of the word, *revival*. Some say that revival is a restoration of God among mankind. Others define it as a destination of God's glory in the church. I prefer to define revival as *passionate life invading the half dead*. No matter your definition, most people will agree that one of the key components of revival is growth. It is an earmark of revival—a sign of health and prosperity.

Where there is a spirit of revival, growth also can be found. In the book of Acts, the Bible says that the Lord *added* to the church daily. The Acts of the apostles was certainly a time of great revival—passionate Christian life was invading a people that were living in half-dead, lifeless religion. Growth was a result of that heavenly invasion. And this time-tested truth has not changed in our day and age; it remains the same—revival brings growth.

Setting the Record Straight

A number of years back we attended a *revival conference*. We were not there to minister, but to be fed. Susie and I were excited to have a chance to sit and receive for a change. During one of the daytime conference meetings, a pastor, one of the conference speakers was scheduled to speak about, *The Effect of Revival*. He began by sharing his story of how revival had come to his local church body a few years previous. He told of all the wonderful miracles that took place during that time, and that it was a truly powerful time in God. He wept as he shared about how revival had transformed his marriage and set his purpose in life back on God's track.

It would have been wonderful had he just stopped there, but he didn't. He went on to confess that two families left the church immediately when the spirit of revival came to his church. He continued explaining that when revival fire was burning at its hottest, four more families, key families, in his church also left. He admitted that they had all left for different reasons, and for the sake of revival, he believed that losing those families was *his cross to bear.* He went on to say that his church was not growing because of revival. Then, like a bow on the top of a present, he closed by making the argument that he would rather have *quality than quantity.*

As I sat there listening to this man speak so disparagingly about the effects of revival, my mind began to reel with scripture after scripture, from the book of Acts, about numerical church growth. Nowhere in the Bible does it ever say we have to exchange quality for quantity. This man never spoke about whether or not his church placed an emphasis on winning the lost to Jesus. He didn't tell us stories of how the people in the church got so engulfed in the fire of God that they couldn't help but take it to their unsaved neighbors, relatives, coworkers, or even to the strangers in the grocery store.

Revival must be caught and then brought. It doesn't require a degree in theological or doctrinal studies in order to multiply. Acts chapter two sets the pattern. The passionate message of Jesus Christ was circulated outside the church walls. Christians viewed themselves as the church. Through them, Jesus Christ was taken house to house. The lost were presented with the living examples of Jesus Christ, and because of that, *"the Lord added to the church daily."*

Do the Math

"Then the word of God spread, and the number of the disciples multiplied greatly in Jerusalem, and a great many of the priests were obedient to the faith" (Acts 6:7 NKJV).

108

In America today, many churches are failing, giving up, and shutting the doors. Obviously, this is not God's desire. Would it not be a wonderful thing to see a church literally on every corner? Would it not be wonderful to have too many churches, rather than too few? Let me share with you some very alarming statistics about the church today.

1. Every day, 10 Christian churches close down in America. Annually, approximately 3,500 close their doors forever.

2. 85% of American Christian churches are in decline of growth.

3. 60,000 Christian churches (1/5) did not report a single convert last year.

4. A 2002 survey revealed that only 6% of American Christian churches were growing numerically.

Believe it! The truth is that if we are not growing, then we are dying. We claim to serve a *Living God*, but many, if not most, churches of every denomination worldwide are found, year after year, standing neck high in a complacent state of stale, lifeless apathy. That numbness eventually leads to deadness within the heart of church leaders, and then into every area of church administration. And the complacency does not stop there. Soon congregants are riddled with the same spiritual disease of apathy as their pastors, priests, and church leaders.

Church leaders begin their Christian work with great passion, purpose, and promise. Many hold onto a prophetic word that was spoken into their lives, confirming what the Holy Spirit planted deep within them years earlier. They enter the ministry with their feet running, full of zeal for the work of the Kingdom of God. The *Spirit of Revival* is so tangible on them that it can be felt when you stand in their presence. They are eaten up with excitement to *save the world*. It is a feeling that they expect to last forever, and then it doesn't. So, what happens along the way?

One of the top reasons for discouragement in ministry is lack of attendance and membership. A staggering eighty-two percent of Christian churches in America claim to have between zero to one community outreach each year. Only nine percent of Christian churches in America admit to hosting more than one outreach to their community annually. *Church as usual* continues. And still, we shake our head and wonder why so many churches are closing down at an alarming rate.

Three Parables of Growth

"He also spoke this parable: A certain man had a fig tree planted in his vineyard, and he came seeking fruit on it and found none. Then he said to the keeper of his vineyard, Look, for three years I have come seeking fruit on this fig tree and find none. Cut it down; why does it use up the ground? But he answered and said to him, Sir, let it alone this year also, until I dig around it and fertilize it. And if it bears fruit, well. But if not, after that you can cut it down" (Luke 13:6-9 NKJV).

This section of scriptures in Luke chapter thirteen is one of my favorite parables. I can see the message of revival laced throughout it. Jesus paints for us the perfect picture of the Christian believer— the fig tree. Obviously, the purpose of a fig tree is to product figs. Then a certain man comes to us time and time again looking to find the fruit we have produced. In this parable, no fruit can be found and He commands that the tree be cut down so that a new tree, a fruit bearing tree, could take its place. My friend, that is REVIVAL!

"Then he said, what is the kingdom of God like? And to what shall I compare it? It is like a mustard seed, which a man took and put in his garden; and it grew and became a large tree, and the birds of the air nested in its branches" (Luke 13:18-19 NKJV).

Here, Jesus uses the illustration of a small *seed.* He says that this seed would *grow* and become *large,* inferring that there should be growth if it is planted in the Kingdom of God. Lack of growth is not an option in the Kingdom of God. From the beginning God says that a seed must produce after its own kind (Genesis 8:22).

When the Kingdom of God is injected, it should always produce fruit and have growth according to the Master. This is true in every situation and circumstance.

Again, using the business world as an example, new growth is common practice for every company, and each employee must strive to assure that the company starts and continues to grow. Budgets and sales goals are determined from pushing every employee to push for more efficiency and greater growth annually. Shareholders of any company stock will make sure that there is plenty of pressure for new growth placed on the leadership of that company. While so many of us are used to this culture Monday through Friday, yet it is a foreign concept within the administration of the church. Why are churches content with the same annual growth, finances, salvations, and discipleship of the congregation, year after year?

"And again He said, "To what shall I liken the kingdom of God? It is like leaven, which a woman took and hid in three measures of meal till it was all leavened" (Luke 13:20 NKJV).

When the measures of leaven was injected into the meal, the whole meal was affected and grew. The Kingdom of God, like the leaven, causes multiplication and growth. The Kingdom is about growth, dominion and taking over.

When the early church in the book of Acts burst forth, the Jewish leaders, even the Caesars, Kings, and Magistrates, were terrified because the believers were filling the earth with their message of the Kingdom. A *dominion mentality* was transforming their cultures, and kingdoms were being influenced by the power of the Cross.

Today, change your thinking about this growing Kingdom. Begin to have a *Kingdom mentality* that will be a growing leaven and seed mentality that will not be unproductive like the fig tree was.

Instead, it will show forth the majesty and glory of our God by a people who want to change the world by the message of the Kingdom. If God could show Himself strong with the spirit of revival in the book of Acts, do you think that He is powerful enough to show the same with you and your church? Capture the revelation today that still, stagnant waters are toxic, but fresh rivers of living water are teaming with LIFE. Produce, multiply, and win the world for Jesus.

Goals and Souls

In the business world, salesmen are encouraged constantly to set goals. Incentives are used to drive their goals to reality, because ultimately the company knows they cannot grow or even exist without sales. The Church would be well advised to follow the example set by the business world, by setting for themselves *faith goals.* Goals for souls.

By setting *faith goals* a church could focus on a specific number of how many people they would like to see added every month to the church. With every *faith goal,* there needs to be a plan—a Holy Spirit strategy to accomplish that goal.

A wonderful pastor friend of ours regularly practices this method. After he powerfully caught a hold of the spirit of revival he began to put the harvest first in his church. With only forty people in his church, he laid before them a challenge—*a faith goal.* They implemented a plan of action to see their church grow. Within ten months, from October to August of the next year, the church grew to over 290 people. That's almost eight-hundred percent growth! God added to their numbers weekly, just like the book of Acts church.

God is a God of increase and multiplication. He believes in it and even His Kingdom is not only an everlasting Kingdom, it is a multiplying Kingdom. God's Kingdom multiplies our finances, multiplies our vision, multiplies our faith, multiplies our knowledge, and multiplies souls into His Kingdom as we stretch our faith to grow with Him. *"And believers were increasingly added to the Lord, multitudes of both men and women"* (Acts 5:14 NKJV). We encourage people to start a home Bible study to see God multiply it with the lost, and then bring those souls with you to your local church for discipleship. To Jesus, outreach was always first, followed by discipleship. Maybe we can learn from the Master plan of outreach and discipleship?

CHAPTER 13
THE ANOINTING

"The anointing in most churches is as rare as chicken's teeth!" – Dr. Rodney Howard-Browne[8]

The awesome presence of God is essential in the life of every Christian. Believe it or not, there are many Christians who are strangers to the powerful manifested presence of God. Maybe they have never been disciplined to know that there is more available in the Kingdom of God. Perhaps, they have just grown cold and lethargic when it comes to the pursuit of God's presence. No matter the reason, we need to have a revelation of the importance of the anointing, the tangible presence of God, and why it is vital for healthy Christian living.

The anointing of God is the Holy Spirit of God, and He has set you apart, sealed you, consecrated and dedicated you, for His Holy purpose. God's anointing must be Holy, precious and more special to you than your next breath. If you have walked with the Holy Spirit for any length of time, you will know that He is the most wonderful gift. There is nothing spooky about Him. He doesn't linger behind the pew or hover over the steeple of the church waiting to come out with a Holy Ghost paddle. He is our friend, our help, our guide, our healer, and oh, so much more.

So much can take place when the Holy Spirit anointing arrives in a place. He can come like a steamroller, bursting through the doors, and He can come like the softest rain. But, no matter how He comes, as we welcome Him, we will be changed every time. He's the softener of men's hearts, and He is the transforming essence of heaven. He is that still small voice, and He is the voice that rings out like a trumpet.

Separated and Dedicated

"And you shall make from these a holy anointing oil, an

ointment compounded according to the art of the perfumer. It shall be a holy anointing oil. With it you shall anoint the tabernacle of meeting and the ark of the Testimony. And you shall speak to the children of Israel, saying: 'This shall be a holy anointing oil to Me throughout your generations" (Exodus 30:25-26, 31 NKJV).

God does nothing without purpose, and the anointing will always accomplish the purposes of God. In Exodus, God gave Moses the specific directions and exact dimensions of the tabernacle and the ark of the Testimony. Then, He gave very specific orders to the priests to make a special anointing oil that would be Holy to the Lord. The word *"Holy"* means *"set apart,"* or *"consecrated, and dedicated for God's use only."* God wanted the anointing oil to be *set apart, dedicated for His use only.*

When I was a young boy, we would often travel to my grandmother's home for visits and holidays. My grandmother was always warm and full of welcoming love. She lived in a large home and one of my favorite things to do was explore room to room of that big, beautiful house. I can distinctly remember a certain room that came with a very specific set of instructions—KEEP OUT. It was my grandmother's formal dining room, and I knew without a shadow of a doubt that this room was off limits to me.

This was a special room, and was only used on very special occasions. In the center of the room sat a large, solid oak table, big enough to seat twelve people. Along the wall was a matching buffet and china hutch, laden with painted gold legs, and plate glass windows. The hutch, I was told, was especially off limits to me.

My grandmother's hutch housed her formal china dishes, her special silverware, and the very special crystal glasses that were wedding gifts to her and grandpa many years ago. This room was unlike any other room in their big house. It was special, it was purposed, set apart, and dedicated for special guests and the most special occasions.

The anointing is special and it is Holy. Like my grandmother's formal dining room, we must learn to treat the anointing with respect

114

and love, giving it the most special care. Yet, unlike my grandmother's formal dining room, the anointing is never off limits to us.

The beautiful revelation about those very specific anointing oil instructions from God to Moses, was that the oil was to be used for God alone. It was not to be used for foolishness or religious traditions—but only used for the purposes of God.

> *"...how God anointed Jesus of Nazareth with the Holy Spirit and with power, who went about doing good and healing all who were oppressed by the devil, for God was with Him"* (Acts 10:38 NKJV).

As in the ministry of Jesus, the function of the anointing is for setting captives free and healing those who are sick and oppressed. The anointing has purpose. God has already given us everything that we need to manifest the supernatural all around us. In the anointing, we have the healing balm that cures afflictions, heavy hearts, broken lives, and shattered people. We have that same anointing, the same power of God as Jesus of Nazareth had. We must not allow the oil of God to become stale for lack of use; instead, we must take the anointing and fire of God out to those who are hurting and bound and in need of the healing touch of God.

Tangibility of the Anointing

> *"Now a certain woman had a flow of blood for twelve years, Immediately the fountain of her blood was dried up, and she felt in her body that she was healed of the affliction. And Jesus immediately knowing in Himself that power had gone out of Him, turned around in the crowd and said, Who touched me"* (Mark 5:25, 29-30 NKJV)?

The anointing is tangible. It can be felt and experienced by our natural senses and our spiritual senses. The story in Mark chapter 5 is one of my favorite Bible stories. It is one of my favorites because it shows so clearly that the anointing of God is tangible—it can be transferred from one individual to another. The story shows that the anointing is alive and moving; it is purposed and ready to work. It shows that the anointing defies our human logic and it is truly a key to the Kingdom of God.

The anointing was not limited to the woman's culture, her circumstances, or her gender. The anointing responded to one thing—her hunger. When she touched the masters garment, she could actually feel the power of God as it surged through her body. The Bible tells us that Jesus could actually feel the power leave Him. Amazingly, the power of God went out of Jesus and into the woman, immediately curing her infirmity.

We see the tangibility of the anointing over and over again throughout the Bible. Jesus would lay his hands on the sick and they would recover. Jesus would spit in the mud and make clay, and placing it in the blind man's eyes, he was able to see. People who were in the path of Peter's shadow were healed. Cloth, anointed by Paul, the Apostle, was placed upon the sick and they were made well. Glory to God!

Horse Posts

While the tangibility to the anointing is found all over scripture, it is also evident throughout church history. In my book, *"Fire That Could Jump the Ocean"* I share about a revivalist in the early 1900s by the name of John G. Lake. He was an insurance salesman who became one of the greatest revivalists. Early in his ministry, John encountered the power of God's anointing and quickly became addicted. Throughout his life and ministry, he took the tangible anointing around the world.

Shortly after his baptism in the Holy Spirit, God stirred in his heart a desire to travel to South Africa. Soon, he boarded a boat with his family, and they embarked on their mission to South Africa to bring this baptism in the Spirit to the people of God on the other side of the ocean.

Day after day, he saw diseases dissolve under his hands, and quickly the word spread to the masses about this man of God. Because of his powerful miracle and healing ministry, John G. Lake pioneered churches wherever he traveled in South Africa.

Once, when John was ministering in the city of Pretoria, he drew such a crowd that by the time he had to leave for the next city, he could not pray for all the people who had come to him. But, Lake had the revelation of the anointing, and he understood that the anointing could be released into an object and then transferred from there to the people. He walked over to a hitching post for the horses and he rubbed his hands all over the post. Then he prophesied to the people, "Whoever touches this post will be healed." Long after Lake had departed, the people still came to touch that post and were healed.

Hallelujah Prison

In the mid-1990s, there were many revivals erupting worldwide. I remember hearing about one revival in the United Kingdom where an Anglican church had been touched with the fire of God and revival had erupted, and people were coming from all over Europe to this move of God.

A local chaplain from the nearby maximum-security prison heard about the revival and was invited to attend. He watched each night as the tangible anointing would flow into every service. Finally, the chaplain decided that he too wanted to receive this anointing. So, he made his way to one of the prayer teams. He said that the person who prayed for him prayed only one word, *more*.

The chaplain felt the flow of the anointing come into his body and before he realized what was happening to him, he was on the floor laughing out of control. The joy of the Lord was rushing through his body and in an instant, he felt years of discouragement and despair leave him. Night after night the chaplain attended the meetings, and night after night he was touched afresh by the Holy Spirit anointing.

Soon he began to get a revelation of the tangibility of the anointing, and he craved it even more in his daily life. One day he went to work at the prison as always. Shortly after he arrived, he realized that something had changed in him—he was happy and full of the joy of God. He thought to himself, "How can I get what's happening out there at the revival to happen in here?" Just then, an inmate knocked on his door. He had come to get counsel and prayer. The chaplain almost erupted with enthusiasm with the opportunity to release what was bubbling up inside of him.

He sat the prisoner down on a chair next to his desk, and he laid his hands gently on the man. He prayed one thing, *"More!"* When he did, the anointing flowed out of him and into the prisoner. Just like the chaplain had done, the prisoner busted out in laughter. He fell out of his chair onto the floor, laughing under the power of God. For twenty minutes the prisoner rolled around the floor laughing out of control.

Finally, the guards came to take him back to the cell. The man was still so drunk in the Spirit that they literally had to drag him along the halls of the prison. All the other prisoners assumed that the man was high on drugs. As he passed by their cells, still being dragged by the guards, the other prisoners called out, "Where did you get the stuff?" The words staggered out of his mouth, "The chaplain's got it!" And one by one, all the prisoners wanted to see the chaplain, and bam, bam, bam, the anointing of the Spirit hit the prisoners and revival erupted in the prison.

Holy Envelopes Batman!

In the mid-1990s, a mighty revival erupted in Pensacola, Florida at Brownsville Assembly of God. People from all backgrounds traveled to attend and partake of the outpouring revival anointing of God. Many people were saved and baptized in the Holy Spirit during that time, and countless Christians were revived with the fresh touch of God. Having had the opportunity to go, I can tell you that it was an amazing display of God's goodness and mercy. To this day, I often dream of those days and times when God visited me so powerfully there.

I was told of a young lady who lived in Pensacola and who had been invited to attended the revival meetings. She was the daughter of a Baptist preacher from Pennsylvania. The first night she attended she was so touched by this tangible anointing that she rededicated her life to Christ and drove home speaking in tongues the whole way back.

She grew so excited and in love with Jesus that she would often call her parents and tell them about what God had done in her heart. Even though they witnessed the fruit of the Spirit maturing in their daughters life, they were still alarmed and concerned that it was too radical and that perhaps what was happening in her was not from the Holy Spirit.

The young lady knew that her parents were not familiar with the anointing of the Holy Spirit and she wanted to show them what was happening during the meetings to help ease their fears and worries. So she bought them some videocassettes to watch of the preaching, worship, and even the water baptisms. She carefully placed the videocassettes in an envelope, labeled it, and sent it to her parent's home in Pennsylvania. Then she waited.

When the mail was delivered to her parents, the father grabbed the envelope out of his mailbox and brought it into the kitchen. He opened the envelope to remove the videocassettes and when he did, he fell to the floor by the power of God. His wife dashed over to her husband to examine what had happened, and she too was slain in the Spirit. There they both lay on the floor laughing and crying under the presence of God. Needless to say, their lives were transformed even before they could watch a single minute of the revival services.

CHAPTER 14
MIRACLES, SIGNS, AND WONDERS

"Therefore we must give the more earnest heed to the things we have heard, lest we drift away. For if the word spoken through angels proved steadfast, and every transgression and disobedience received a just reward, how shall we escape if we neglect so great a salvation, which at the first began to be spoken by the Lord, and was confirmed to us by those who heard Him, God also bearing witness both with signs and wonders, with various miracles, and gifts of the Holy Spirit, according to His own will" (Hebrews 2:1-4 NKJV)?

I knew that I had become a radical revivalist when I stepped out of my toasty warm rental car and into unbearably cold weather of Alberta, Canada. The temperature outside was a breathtaking forty-five degrees below zero. It was the kind of cold that freezes your lungs with every inhale of breath. It was winter and I was scheduled to preach for a couple weeks in a church located just outside the limits of Edmonton.

I was a bit surprised to see that despite the freezing temperature, the local people were pouring into the church. Where I come from, folks do not dare to leave the safety and warmth of their home at the slightest cold front or at the mildest snow fall forecast. But, these spiritually hungry people were out for something.

Each night, the church was packed with hungry people who were desperate for an encounter with the power of God. The miracles and healings increased daily, and every night, new people would testify about being filled with the power and glory of God. The final service was dedicated to be, *Miracle Night*, and the people from the church were inviting everyone they could think of to join us for one last powerful night of miracles. One young women, a member of the church, desperately wanted her husband to join her. Day after day, the young woman begged her husband to attend the revival meetings with her, and day after day he would refuse. He was a professed atheist. Since becoming a Christian her love for God grew deeper, while his denial of God, unbending. The day before the final night, she approached me in the foyer of the church just as I was bundling up to leave. At her desperate urging, we agreed together in prayer, "Lord, may this woman find favor with her husband when she returns home tonight and invites him one last time."

It was *Miracle Night* and the church was packed to capacity. Some were resigned to sitting on the floor of the isles of the church; others were propped up into the window sills. I looked out over the crowd and there, in the back of the church, sat this precious young woman and beside her was her husband. His arms were crossed in defiance, but he was there. Yes, this was truly, *Miracle Night.*

The service began as usual. The praise and worship started and the anticipation was higher than any other night. Manifestations of the Holy Spirit started right from the beginning as people were on their knees in worship—weeping and crying out to God all around the altar.

After worship ended I began to preach. I sensed the Holy Spirit pulling me toward miracles and after my message was delivered, I called for all the sick people to come forward. Immediately, people were being healed and touched with the fire of God. A short while later I looked around; bodies were strewn all over the building. Some were under the pews; some were draped over the top of the pews. It looked like a Holy Spirit bomb had exploded.

I prayed for all the sick people, and then I called forward anyone who wanted to receive a fresh encounter with God. I had already laid hand on hundreds, but as I looked up, I noticed there were two people left standing who wanted prayer. One was an elderly woman and the other was a young teenaged girl standing toward the back of the church.

I prayed for the older lady in the middle of the center isle of the church, and as I did, the power of God struck the young teenaged girl in the back of the church. The girl was propelled through the air and landed four rows back—right near the atheist man. The people around her gasped. I was stunned—like the rest of them, but I told the church, "God started it, let Him finish it." We had all just witnessed a powerful God show up in the midst of His hungry people, but no one was ready for what was about to happen next.

When the teenager was launched through the air, she landed and lay there under the power of God. The atheist man was a paramedic by trade, and when he saw how the girl had been lifted up and launched through the air, he jumped to his feet and ran to her aid. He expected to find her with a terrible injury, but instead, she was laughing and smiling under the power of God. He carefully repositioned her body thinking perhaps she had experienced a head injury or that she was delusional or unconscious. As he moved her she laughed even louder. Just then, the anointing that was on her, jumped on him! He stood up straight as an arrow under the fear of God, and he walked quickly back to his seat. He turned to his wife and said, "There's an unseen power on that girl over there."

When I returned home, the pastor of the church called to tell me the wonderful news. The young woman's atheist husband was so moved by the God's powerful sign and wonder that he gave his life to Christ and was radically born-again. Today, he serves as the deacon of the church.

"So great fear came upon all the church and upon all who heard these things. And through the hands of the apostles many signs and wonders were done among the people. And they were all with one accord in Solomon's Porch. Yet none of the rest dared join them, but the people esteemed them highly. And believers were increasingly added to the Lord, multitudes of both men and women, so that they brought the sick out into the streets and laid them on beds and couches, that at least the shadow of Peter passing by might fall on some of them" (Acts 5:11-15 NKJV).

God does nothing by accident or coincidence. Everything that He does is done with purpose. When signs and wonders occur, they give us an opportunity to experience great awe and deeper love for God.

Let me share a statistic that was done by sociologists in reference to people who had attended the revival meetings in Toronto, Canada during the Toronto Blessing of the 1990's. Sociologists tested 1,000 people who had experienced documented signs or wonders. As a result of their experience with signs or wonders, 93% said they loved God more, and over 85% were compelled to share their experience with others, encouraging them to attend and experience the outpouring of God's power also.

Two-fold Purpose

During my years of ministry experience, I've learned that signs and wonders serve a two-fold purpose to people, saved and unsaved alike. God uses them as *pathfinders* to help bring people to Him or bring people closer to Him. Secondly, God uses signs and wonders as *heart revealers.* By opening up and revealing a person's heart, they are better able to examine what abides within them and come to the place of repentance. Of course, God has given each of us the ability to accept or to reject His goodness brought through His signs and wonders, but it is always the goodness of God that leads us to repentance.

Anytime a miracle occurs, it holds us to a higher standard of belief and yielding to the Kingdom of God. Every miracle shows us the invasion from another world—a world where the demonstrations of miracles, signs, and wonders is normal.

The Biblical Greek word, *signs* is "semeion," which means "a supernatural token." And the Biblical Greek word, *wonders* is "teras," which means "unexplainable phenomena, supernatural prodigies, omens, unusual manifestations and acts that are so unusual that they cause the observer to marvel in awe."

Signs are like signposts pointing mankind toward God. They are not our *destination,* they are our *directions.* When you look for a restaurant to dine, you begin by looking for the sign. Once you arrive at the restaurant, you do not just stop and stand in front of the sign, you go in and eat. The sign only pointed the way for you.

The only thing predictable about godly signs is that they are unpredictable. By their very nature, signs must to be unique in order to stand out. They are usually unprecedented. Moses performed signs that had never before been done, as did Elijah and Jesus.

"And it shall come to pass That whoever calls on the name of the Lord Shall be saved.' "Men of Israel, hear these words: Jesus of Nazareth, a Man attested by God to you by miracles, wonders, and signs which God did through Him in your midst, as you yourselves also know" (Acts 2:21-22 NKJV).

Carnal Christianity

Carnal Christianity denounces signs and wonders of God. The carnal church does not welcome them, but resorts to mocking and ridiculing, making no place for them to occur. The carnal church, much like the Gnostics of the first century, equates knowledge with spirituality. It says that anything exterior or that deals with the body of mankind is wicked and sinful. It elevates intellectualism, and demotes any exterior experience.

The Gnostics taught that there is salvation in knowledge and godly wisdom, and that any experience that we have with God, must come through our minds, not our bodies. Analytical intellectualism is exalted as a higher type of spirituality.

The Apostle John dealt strongly with these people in most of his writings because they were constantly trying to ridicule what God did through Jesus. So in his first gospel John writes, *"In the beginning was the word, and the word became FLESH..."* (John 1:1 KJV). John is bringing to light that the intellectual gospel is not from God. In order to help them consider the vastness of the exterior workings of Jesus, John concludes his gospel writing with these words, *"And there are also many other THINGS that Jesus did, which if they were written on by one, I suppose that even the world itself could not contain the books that would be written. Amen"* (John 21:25 NKJV).

Knowledge alone does not deliver people. We know that God delivered Israel from Egypt with signs and wonders, not through knowledge (Deuteronomy 26:8; Acts 7:36). In Acts 5:12, we learn that, *"Through the hands of the apostles many signs and wonders were done among the people."* The entire ministry of Jesus was earmarked with signs and wonders, and at the same time, the Bible teaches us that His Church would be discernible by signs and wonders.

Biblical Signs

I began an in-depth study on the Biblical precedent of signs and wonders. I was awestruck as to what I learned and my theology was stretched with greater revelation of God's ability to reveal His self to mankind. Signs and wonders transcend centuries and even the Old and New Testaments. They were not limited to just the Israelites, just to men, or just with those who believed.

In Acts 4:31 when the early church prayed, they had an earthquake. In Acts 12:23, Herod had elevated himself in pride and because of that he was struck by an angel and eaten alive by worms. In Luke 1:19-20, Zacharias was struck dumb by an angel before the birth of his son, John the Baptist. In the book of Acts we learn that as the cripples were laid in Peter's shadow they were healed and their paralysis and other ailments left. In the Old Testament, God anointed a donkey to speak to a man of God and in the New Testament miracle money was found in the mouth of a fish.

The very first miracle of Jesus was recorded in the second chapter of John—He turned the water into wine. The children of Israel were led out of the desert by a pillar of cloud and a pillar of fire. Jonah, the prophet, was swallowed by a great fish for three days and three nights. These are not *stories* that we tell our children. They are not fables made up by the minds of men, these are *actual* and *factual* accounts of God moving in signs and wonders to touch and change men's lives.

When the Word of God comes with power, it causes people to trust in God's ability and shows the infallible proof that He loves them. *"For our gospel did not come to you in word only, but also in power, and in the Holy Spirit and in much assurance, as you know what kind of men we were among you for your sake"* (1 Thessalonians 1:5 NKJV).

Powerful Signs After Pentecost

Contrary to some denominational, theological and doctrinal stances, God did not conclude with signs, wonders, or miracles, after the apostles. As we look back to Acts chapter 2, when the day of Pentecost had fully come, on through to today, we see that history highlights certain men and women that have been strongly and strangely used by God, earmarking their ministry with signs, wonders, and miracles.

Revivalist William Branham had so many strange signs and wonders throughout his ministry. Angelic appearances and visitations, the dead being raised, supernatural sightings of fire and halo's appearing in photographs are only a few of many that he experienced. It was common that because of the strong current of the power of God flowing through his hands that his wristwatch would explode. He would often times have to remove it before he would lay his hands on the people.

Revivalist John G. Lake, was known to have so many strange signs and wonders in his ministry that he could not even shake hands with the visitors at the door of the church because they would fall out, under the power in heaping piles. On one occasion, the power of God was so strong though him that burn marks appeared on people's bodies where he had just laid his hand.

Evangelist Maria Woodworth-Etter was a woman known for the signs and wonders that followed her ministry. In her book, *Signs and Wonders,* she explains how she stepped up to the platform to preach one day and stretching out her hand she went into a trance. She didn't move for three days. Day and night she stood like an immovable statute. She became known as the *Trance Evangelist* because so many people would fall into trances during her meetings.

Because of all the signs and wonders in her life and ministry, she witnessed multitudes of sinners rushing to get saved everywhere she went.

Show Us Your Glory

"For all the promises of God in Him are Yes, and in Him Amen, to the glory of God THROUGH US" (2 Corinthians 1:20 NKJV).

The demonstrations of the Holy Spirit are absolutely necessary to show forth the Glory of God through us. Let us cry out to God like the early church did in Acts chapter 4, *"By stretching out Your hand to heal, and that signs and wonders may be done through the name of Your holy Servant Jesus"* (Acts 4:30 NKJV).

You are the very glory of God. You have been made new, righteous, holy and perfect, because of the sacrifice of Jesus. In you, God has planted His Kingdom. It may have been planted as a small seed, but it will bloom as a mighty oak tree—a beautiful fig tree that will bear much fruit for the Father. God has made you to be His glory, *"the light, the city on a hill that cannot be hidden"* (Matthew 5). When men see it, they will run to you and be saved.

Just as it was for Paul the Apostle, Revivalist John G. Lake, Evangelist Maria Woodworth-Etter, and so many others, this is your time. Signs, wonders, and miracles are your destiny. You are alive today to show forth the goodness of God in the earth. You have a divine destiny to be Christ Jesus to all those around you. The world is not groaning for better Christmas pageants, or more silk-robed choirs. No, the earth is groaning and the Bible says that it groans and waits with great expectation for the glorious revealing of the sons of God to be made manifest!

Because of our wonderful Lord Jesus, you also are a son of the Most High, Living God. You are commissioned by Him to go forth into the world and manifest His Kingdom through signs, wonders, and miracles. The time for waiting is over. You already have it. You already have Jesus, and the wonderful gift of the Holy Spirit. The earth is your inheritance. Shake off the dust of complacency, and tear through the veil of tradition and religious rituals. Take a hold of it now, be set aflame—and burn with God's Holy fire.

ENDNOTES

Chapter 1. Show Us Your Glory!

1. *"The Touch of God and the Anointing"* Series, Rodney Howard Browne, Written Permission granted.

2. ibid
3. ibid

Chapter 2. Quit Playing In Your Food

4. ibid

Chapter 9. Passion, Out of Control

5. ibid
6. ibid

Chapter 11. Don't Touch My Treasure!

7. ibid

Chapter 13. The Anointing

8. ibid

About
THE AUTHOR

Tom & Susie Scarrella

Tom Scarrella is the founder/president of *Scarrella Ministries*, an international traveling ministry based out of Fort Lauderdale, Florida. Tom is also the founder and director of *Ministry Training Institute* (MTI), a correspondence based ministry training program. In addition, Tom and his wife, Susie, host and produce their own weekly television program, *"All for the Kingdom,"* which airs in over 200 million homes around the globe.

At the HEART of *Scarrella Ministries*, revival burns. It is their passion to see the body of Jesus Christ fervently set ablaze with Grace, Truth, Miracles, and with the Power of God, reaching out to a lost world to establish the Kingdom of God among men.

Beginning in the ministry in 1986, Tom pastored until 1994 when after transitioning their entire ministry, he founded *Scarrella Ministries* and began traveling worldwide igniting revival fires. Since their marriage in 2003, together Tom and Susie, have ministered in over twenty nations and in every one of the United States of America.

Since their ministry's inception, they have continued to minister with a strong emphasis on *Revival, Passion, and the Power of God.* As a ministry, since 2003 they have been witness to a mighty increase in miracles, signs, and wonders as unlike any other time in the history of Scarrella Ministries. As a result, thousands have been healed from blindness, deafness, lameness, and diseases. And just as with the commission of the early disciples, SIGNS and WONDERS follow their ministry.

"And my speech and my preaching was not with enticing words of man's wisdom, but in demonstration of the Spirit and of power: That your faith should not stand in the wisdom of men, but in the power of God."

-- I Corinthians 2:4-5

Tom Scarrella Ministries
www.SHAREtheFIRE.org
phone 954-336-5993

132